You Are the One

Leigh and Roy,

what a great place you
chose for retirement!

Best wishes for many years
of health and happiness.

Jim

You Are the One

Achieving More Happiness
and Success

Sam Daniel Jr.

Writers Club Press
San Jose New York Lincoln Shanghai

You Are the One
Achieving More Happiness and Success

Writers Club Press
an imprint of iUniverse.com, Inc.

For information address:
iUniverse.com, Inc.
620 North 48th Street, Suite 201
Lincoln, NE 68504-3467
www.iuniverse.com

ISBN: 0-595-01120-9

Printed in the United States of America

To Dad, Robbye, and Mona for your love and care in making my life brighter

You can change your life by changing your thinking.

William James

Contents

Acknowledgments

I would like to thank the following individuals for their input, perspective, support, encouragement, and understanding during the writing of this book: my wife and friend for forty years, Robbye; my encouraging daughter, Mona; my friend and writer, Joan Fouhy; my friend and sister-in-law, Judy Heichel, and my friend and associate, Nick Zangari.

Your support and interest have been invaluable.

Introduction

As you will read in Chapter One, you are the *one*. You are special and you deserve the best life you can live. You have the power to influence your future by choosing your way through, or around, conditions or obstacles in your way. If you want to improve the quality of your life and achieve more satisfaction and success, this book can help.

I wrote the book because I believe that too many individuals don't seem to recognize their uniqueness or their power to control many of the outcomes affecting them. They don't feel that they can control their attitudes, moods, feelings, or careers. Some are victims of self-induced helplessness and are bored, frustrated, or resigned to their unsatisfactory situations. Others remain in jobs, relationships, or situations that they don't want. As a result, they don't feel either happy or successful. Even if they recognize that different decisions can lead to better results for them, they seem unable to make those key decisions. They are procrastinating despite their pain or frustration.

I believe there is a better way, and I want to try to help those who are stuck in frustration and indecision or who want a better life. One of the central messages of this book is that life is too important and too brief to merely dread or endure. During the Vietnam War as I witnessed injuries and deaths, I realized how precious and fleeting life could be. While in Vietnam, I resolved never to take life or health for granted again. I was so thankful to return safely that I decided to try to influence others to make the most of their lives while they could. I've tried to honor that obligation since 1967, when I returned. This book is part of that ongoing commitment.

The ideas and suggestions are practical, and the topics should be applicable to some aspects of your situation. The chapters are based on real life situations or experiences. During the past thirty-eight years, as a military officer, manager, and senior executive, I've led platoons, companies, operational units, departments, and divisions. In those roles, I've mentored hundreds of individuals, including presidents, in various organizations. Further, I have experienced, or have seen other people experience, many of the problems, challenges, hardships, misfortunes, or crises that you might face. During the years, I've noticed the contrast in approaches used by successful and unsuccessful individuals to address their problems, challenges, or misfortunes. Their attitudes made the difference. Some became better while others only became bitter. Some bounced back, learned from the setbacks, and became even happier and more successful. However, others with similar troubles remained negative and unsuccessful, and they never overcame their bitterness. They had not learned that misery is optional.

Also, since my first job in business, I've been interested in how people become successful and what makes the difference in thought and motivation between those who do and those who don't achieve success. I started reading books on success, observed successful achievers, and was fortunate to have successful mentors along the way. As a result of this learning experience, I've been fortunate to develop and to achieve more than I could have without that valuable knowledge and exposure. In addition to my own positive experience with these approaches, I've seen them applied successfully by others. Therefore, I'm a believer, and I can attest to the difference these ideas and approaches can make in your life.

However, you define your own happiness and success because you're the only one who really knows how you feel about your life at any given point. Also, you know where you started, how far you've come, and what challenges you had to overcome along the way. Additionally, you have to know your own mind and values, or you'll be influenced to seek what others want for you. Knowing yourself is key. You know when you feel authentic and real and when you feel like a phony. Do you know yourself? Do you feel authentic, happy, and successful? How do you measure happiness and success? A wise person observed that success is getting what you want, while happiness is wanting what you get. You can achieve more of both by learning to think differently.

The ideas, suggestions, philosophy, and the additional reading list in the Appendix can help if you've experienced or are experiencing some of the following situations. They apply if you are:

- Feeling that there's more to life than you're currently experiencing
- Trying to strengthen your self-esteem or gain more confidence
- Trying to become more successful in your work or profession
- Confused about the direction of your life or career
- Not feeling optimistic about your future
- Putting yourself down with negative self-talk
- Not feeling special or important
- Trying to bounce back from a setback or loss
- Feeling stuck in a rut and needing a change
- Avoiding or delaying decisions that you know you need to make
- Trying to adjust to being fired, laid off, or retired early
- Coping with threats to your career
- Feeling trapped in a relationship, marriage, or job
- Trying to regain your enthusiasm and faith in your future
- Managing employees and trying to motivate them or to correct some attitude and performance problems
- Complaining and exhibiting a negative attitude

This book can help you address some of the above issues. The ideas, thoughts, and suggestions in the book do work and can help you change if you apply them. If you're willing to spend the time reading, reflecting, and acting on your decisions, you can change.

Although there is some overlap among the chapters, each one covers a different subject. I recommend that you read the first chapter and then scan the others for topics of interest. Also, the Table of Contents and the Index can point to you to specific subjects. I hope the book will be an ongoing reference. It can help you from time-to-time because you will probably experience some of the challenges more than once.

I wish I could guarantee that these thoughts, ideas, and suggestions would absolutely work for you. However, I can't provide a guarantee because so much of the outcome depends on you. Your willingness to address some of your issues or situations is the key to making this book work for you. This statement is based on my experience as a leader, speaker, and friend in trying to influence others to change.

Some individuals I advised were frustrated and ready for change. As a result, they seized the new ideas and perspective, changed their thinking, and achieved better lives. Others, unfortunately, who were equally frustrated, got excited temporarily but made no effort to change, and they remained stuck in place. To help, I can point out some ideas, philosophy, and resources, but only you can decide if you're willing to take the time and make the effort to be happier and more successful. But, if you're ready, then some of these thoughts and ideas might seem like fresh oxygen when you're short of breath.

I've heard just about every reason why people don't change, but if you want to alter your situation enough, you'll find a way to do it. When you're motivated, your ability to overcome obstacles is incredible. Conversely, if you want to make excuses for not even trying, you can find an endless supply. Basically, you either want something enough or you don't. The clock is still running on your life, whether you do or you don't make any changes. The reality is that your obituary will be printed either way. Until then, it's up to you to live the life you want.

Your life is precious and you can choose to live with happiness and fulfillment, boredom and indifference, or bitterness and regret. You may experience some bad breaks along the way, but you can control your reaction to those misfortunes. With a positive attitude, those unexpected setbacks might slow you down, but you can recover and stay on track to your goals.

Since we can't meet face-to-face, I will encourage you through these words. You only live once, and you have a chance to make the most of your life. Don't let your epitaph read, "I could have, but I didn't." You hold the key to any changes you want to make. Although I will offer some ideas and suggestions, *you* have to make it happen. By changing your thinking and attitude, you can literally begin to see the world through different eyes. Subsequent chapters will expand on the idea of "seeing" differently.

In urging you to seize control over your future, I will be blunt on some points. The reason for bluntness is that it's sometimes difficult to get others to make significant changes with gentle nudges, because it's so easy for them to put off difficult decisions. Therefore, I'll *stress* the importance of your decisions and your actions following those decisions. Your choices can make such a difference for you that I make no apology for advocating that you make them. Further, certain themes or statements are repeated throughout the book. They are important to remember and are worth repeating.

Although your situation might be different, I've found that some individuals, despite being unhappy at work or at home, still remain in a comfort zone. Their situation might be frustrating or irritating, but it's not uncomfortable *enough* to trigger change. Occasionally, they blow off steam to relieve pressure, but, despite their recurring irritation, anger or sadness, they remain in their frustrating situation. Their friends, relatives, and associates can't believe that they complain and remain, but they do. They don't realize that their limitations might be imaginary. Comfort zones are seductive. They can keep you in situations that you don't like and want to change.

You have to wake up, see your situation for what it is, and start changing to reach your goals. Who is stopping you? You have to provide that *extra* drive and impetus to change your situation because you can be too close to your problem to resolve it. For example, you can be like a boxer in a clinch. With his arms wrapped around the other fighter, he is too close to throw an effective punch. You might be so entangled with your issue that you lack the perspective to make a good decision. If you put some distance between you and your dilemma, get some rest, and reflect on the matter at hand, you can get a running start at the problem. Distance, perspective, and rest can build your resolve to decide and to act.

However, if you're on the treadmill of indecision, you have to remind yourself that a treadmill won't take you anywhere, and you will probably stay on yours until you *decide* and get off. Also, is it realistic to expect someone to come and rescue you or to resolve your dilemma for you? If *you* don't decide and act to resolve your situation, you can waste years of your life just existing and tolerating what you don't like. Don't ever forget your power to change your situation. If you find yourself complaining frequently about your situation, then use that same energy to choose a different outcome. Generally, unproductive complaining only makes you more miserable and doesn't solve your problem. Realistically, what will make tomorrow any different, if you don't start doing something different today?

Why dread or endure your situation, when you can live a full and enjoyable life? You're a special person and you deserve better. But, you have to want it enough to do something about it. With this book, I've tried to get you started on the road to an even better life. I wish you every success on that journey.

Sam Daniel Jr.
Williamsburg, Virginia

Chapter One

Successful from the Beginning

You've been successful from the beginning. You overcame incredible odds to even be born. Starting among *millions* of sperm seeking to fertilize a single egg, you were the one to reach life. To be that one, your odds were higher than those required to win a state lottery—and, you know how impossible those odds seem.

Since you overcame such odds to even be here, you're strong enough to handle any challenges while you're here. Because your life is so rare and special, you should resolve to *live* every day and to cherish each breath and heartbeat. Each of your days is a once-in-a-lifetime experience, and you should make the most of each one. Although you're fortunate to have a life, *you* have to make it worth living.

Unfortunately, some people are still waiting for life to make them happy. Usually, happiness and success don't happen by accident, and your life is too precious to spend being bored, indecisive, helpless, or miserable. You can avoid these negative conditions if you're open to some different information and perspective.

This book can help you achieve more happiness and success if you're willing to consider some changes in your thinking. As I stated in the Introduction, Vietnam intensified my appreciation of life, and I've been

1

thankful every day since returning safely. This book is part of my continuing commitment to help you value your life and to live it with more satisfaction and success.

Over the years, I've been fortunate to work with many employees, from trainees to chief executives. During that experience, I've seen the positive changes that result from improved perspective, attitude, commitment, and effort. In addition, I've experienced these positive changes in my own life and have observed similar results among many others. As a result of seeing those changes, I believe you can realize your potential if your desire, drive, and discipline are strong enough. With more faith, focus, confidence, and effort, you can improve your life significantly. If you change your limiting thoughts and beliefs, it's still not too late to realize some of your dreams and aspirations. If others can do it, so can you.

Even if you feel trapped in a personal or work situation that appears hopeless, there is usually a way out. Sometimes you can't see the answer because, like an overcast day, your dark clouds of frustration and disappointment temporarily block your view. The sun is still shining above the clouds, and your answer is there, even if it's obscured at the moment. You will find it. But, if you get discouraged, remember these words from W. Clement Stone: "Think, think, think. Never give up. Think it through. The answer is there. You will get your answer if you keep on thinking without panic, without fear of failure. If you learn to recognize and bypass emotional reactions and stress cool, rational thinking, you can think your way out of any trouble or ineffective living."

You've worked your way through difficult situations before. With experience, you've learned that everything passes, eventually, and life goes on. Even under your most challenging conditions, you still control the choices that control your future. You are too valuable to merely exist by "accepting" unsatisfactory conditions in your life. You can change many of those conditions. Choice is not always easy, but it is your passport to better conditions and away from bad situations.

Value Yourself and Your Life

Value yourself and your life, and you are more likely to succeed. You were born to achieve, to enjoy life, and to contribute while you're here. Your life was neither imposed as a penalty nor intended as an ordeal. Instead, if you treat life as a gift, you have value despite your current status or condition. You have intrinsic value by *being*. You entered this world with value and you still have it. Your job, marriage, or financial status doesn't determine your self-worth. But, when you link your self-image to success at work, your skill level, marital status, or your financial resources, you can—mistakenly—feel like a failure if some aspects aren't going well at the moment. Keep reminding yourself of your value, ability, and potential as you read.

Live Your One Life

If you could live forever, it wouldn't matter if you wasted some years due to lack of direction or purpose. However, as you realize at some stage, you only live once. Are you living productively? Do you have specific plans? Are they in writing? Writing forces you to clarify your thinking. If your plans are not written, are they specific enough to motivate you? Do you even know what you want? If you don't know, how do you tell if you don't have it? Also, are you unwittingly making more plans for dying than for living? It's not uncommon for someone to have life insurance, a will, an estate plan—even a burial plot in some cases—but no clear plans for living. When you set positive goals and plans, you won't be drifting and wondering why you don't feel more alive.

Your power and energy need the clarity and focus of goals. Fuzzy intentions don't generate much motivation or enthusiasm. To see the power of focus, take a magnifying glass into the sunlight. Place it above your hand and move the glass until a tiny beam of sunlight is focused on your skin. In seconds, the heat will be so intense that you can't keep your hand there. Further, if you focus the sunlight on a pile of leaves, you can start a fire. Focus is powerful; narrow yours and use it to fire your enthusiasm and energy. If you aim your life with more care, you can be more satisfied and successful.

Unfortunately, many people are confused. They lack a sense of direction, and they haven't recognized their uniqueness or potential. Those without dreams, goals, and plans can settle for boring and unsuccessful jobs, loves, and lives. Expect more from yourself and life. Seek what you deserve and don't settle for less. As you proceed, however, it's helpful to understand why some people don't change, despite their pain or frustration, so you can avoid their frustrations.

Why Some Don't Change

Some don't change due to their comfortable, boring habits. Boredom results from the same old, same old routine. Our familiar and comfortable routines form the thoughts, actions, and habits that become our ruts. A rut has been described as a grave with both ends open. Once we settle into our ruts, it takes guts to leave them. Unfortunately, some never leave their well-worn ruts, and their spirits die years before they do. Those comfortable habits are seductive; they start out thin as the thread of a spider's web, but, with time and repetition, they can seem as strong as steel cable. Those who've tried to break their habits understand the power and hold of their habitual actions.

Others don't change because they don't know what they want. They know the burning itch of frustration, but they don't know where to begin. However, to the dismay of their friends, family, and associates, they can describe their anger, fear, and frustration with clarity and emotion. But, when a friend or loved one asks the inevitable question, "Well, what do you want?" they often admit they don't know. They haven't devoted enough time or analysis to their situation. Until they do, they are only peddling their frustrations in place like a stationary bike. Rarely does anything change until you act or you are forced to act. Sometimes, action is similar to riding an elevator. Have you ever stepped into an elevator alone and realized after a few minutes that it wasn't moving? You had failed to push the button. When you push the button in your life, you take action. But, when you delay, someone on another floor, or in another part of your life, might push the button before you do. Then, like the elevator, your direction responds to the other person's signal first. Don't wait. Don't allow others to push your buttons for you. Take the initiative. There are answers for you and help available to find them.

Some others already know what they want, but they hesitate to change. They are undermined by well-meaning friends and relatives who "help" by emphasizing all the pitfalls and problems ahead. Unfortunately, by playing the devil's advocate, they can reinforce the doubts and fears of the ones involved and stifle their resolve to change. Admittedly, it's a thin line between legitimate caution and excessive concern. But, when individuals allow outside influences to divert them from their calling, they risk having their unrealized dreams die with them. It's sad but true; cemeteries and memorial parks contain too many examples of dreams that never were.

Why don't people develop a vision of what they want and change when they're unhappy? A psychologist friend once said, "When the pain exceeds the pleasure, people will change." However, I've seen many people tolerate high levels of pain before they were forced to change for relief. Some people absorbed more pain than I could believe, and they still wouldn't change. As long as they keep on doing what they are doing, they will keep getting the same, frustrating results. If they don't change, they can eventually become emotionally numb and lose their spirit. They can seriously impair their mental health *if they keep doing what isn't working* long enough.

You Can Change

The good news is that you can change. If you feel frustrated or stymied, you can change by creating goals and plans that inspire a sense of anticipation. Life without anticipation is not exciting. Even hope, itself, is based on future expectations. You need faith in the future to have power in the present. Build your faith, anticipation, and excitement by setting specific goals and plans.

To create a brighter future, you probably already know what you need to do. Sometimes, your solution is to do the obvious. One of your major challenges is bridging the gap between your knowledge and your action. Acting on what you know is critical to your success. You have control over most of the decisions you need to make. Within thirty minutes, you could probably list the key decisions that could change your life (take some time to list them now). If you can list these decisions, why not make them?

If you can't think of any major decisions you need to make, start listing situations or people that are bothering you. After each one, ask yourself if there are any others. If you listen quietly, your inner voice will indicate if there are any more. As a final check to see if you've uncovered the main obstacles to your happiness, say to yourself, "Other than for those reasons on my list, I am fine." Any final issues should surface after this statement. But, if you haven't made decisions on those you did list, you probably lack the conviction or the will to decide. In the absence of conviction and a burning desire to change, you aren't "fired-up" enough to decide or to act on your decision. Why remain upset over situations that you can change with a decision?

Admittedly, it's not easy to change. It requires the time to think, the will to do some soul-searching, and the courage to act on your insights and conclusions. In this process, you might have to change some deeply ingrained thoughts and behaviors that are holding you back. Further, you may even have to leave some friends, environments, or limiting relationships to achieve your goals. Unconsciously, you can adopt some of the thought and behavior patterns of your group. If your associates are not satisfying your needs for growth and success, then it might be time for a change.

Many individuals have become successful after leaving limiting relationships or situations. They found others who believed in them, or, at least, they broke the hold of negative influences on them. If you are facing a negative relationship or situation, a decision to leave can be one of the most difficult choices you ever have to make. But, it can make all the difference in the rest of your life.

I believe in relationships, but if individuals become less by being with each other, it's not fair to either one to continue. It's sad to see good people pass up passion, enthusiasm, happiness, and success only because they could never break away from a negative environment or relationship. Only those who have left negative environments can ever know the better life on the other side of the pain and frustration. However, there are no guarantees for happiness after a change, because so much depends on the quality of subsequent decisions on new relationships, environments, or jobs. Some remain unhappy even after multiple jobs, marriages, or relationships. Only you can decide if your situation is serious enough to justify a major change in your life and direction, and if you're ready for the emotional and financial consequences of that change.

Be Open to Advice but Maintain Control

Although there is plenty of advice and counsel available, you have to sort through it to find your way. It's your life and your future. Only you can decide if your frustration or pain is worth the time, effort, and discomfort to try to change. When you start to change, you, alone, will feel the strain, the emotional ups-and-downs, and the eventual relief afterwards. This is the hard, effective way to change. It might be tempting to take an easier, less effective way. That temptation could be to change nothing, continue to drift, or allow someone else to control your destiny.

To realize your goals, you cannot leave your direction to others, no matter how well-intentioned they are. Although some advice and counsel can be invaluable and might help you avoid some serious problems, you need to know the difference in the quality of advice you accept. It's your life, and you're the only one who can live it; to live it well, you need to take some risks.

Risks Are Part of Change and Success

To be successful, you have to take some risks and walk through a few invisible doors to your future. I use the word *invisible* because it exists only in your mind. Although you can analyze the risks of some decisions in advance, you cannot know the consequences until after you decide and pass through your "mental" door. Often, the answers or solutions are only revealed to you, after you've crossed that threshold of uncertainty. Don't pass up opportunities because of uncertainty. Unfortunately, I've seen bright, competent people hesitate at key decision points and pass up relationships, marriages, promotions, transfers, or other opportunities. They were afraid to walk through those invisible doors and to chance life on the other side.

Risk and chance are part of our successful heritage. For example, consider the fears and risks faced by the early immigrants to America and the settlers on wagon trains heading west. Those courageous travelers apparently weren't worrying if there were a health or dental plan at the new location, when they were taking such chances for better opportunities. Those men and women probably had similar feelings to those described by Paul Tournier when he wrote: "There is an astonishing contrast between the heavy perplexity that inhibits before the adventure has begun and the excitement that grips us the moment it begins. As soon as a man makes up his mind to take the plunge into adventure, he is aware of a new strength he did not think he had, which rescues him from all his perplexities."

Today, unfortunately, many in society have become so security conscious that they forget that the only *real* security is within them. The human spirit's ability to change, risk, sacrifice, and achieve is almost miraculous. Achievers are amazed by what they can accomplish when they risk enough to trigger their survival instincts.

If you risk entering that "door," you'll soon discover that the other side isn't populated with supermen and superwomen, just those who had the courage to enter. For example, how many times have you observed someone become financially independent or more successful than you, when you felt that you were smarter or better qualified than that person? What made the difference? The other person just decided, acted, risked, worked, and achieved. You can do the same, and if one door doesn't open, there are others to try. As you attempt more, you'll see more opportunities. By risking, you can enliven yourself, build your confidence, and achieve much more than by taking a fearful, cautious approach. Although risking can make you nervous, you cannot grow without stretching.

Most achievers have some doubts at times, but they manage them. Doubts can grow with attention and nurturing. Positive individuals have discovered that if they don't "feed" their doubts with attention, the doubts wither. Also, someone wisely recommended that you starve your doubts and feed your faith.

Admittedly, there is risk with change, and the process is not easy. The adage, "No gain without pain," certainly applies to your efforts to change. Make your gain worth the pain and effort.

Power Begins with Concentrated Effort

In directing and controlling your life, where are you now? Are you focused or fuzzy about your future? Unless you clarify your values, needs, and aims and focus your attention and energy, you cannot concentrate enough power to reach your goals. Think of your energy as steam. You can let it evaporate uselessly from an open pot, as with no goals or plans, or you can concentrate it into a powerful force. Instead of steam pipes, you use focused goals to concentrate your energy.

Think and plan more of your life, and you will feel a stronger sense of direction and progress. You're better off with this approach than by drifting and hoping something better will come along. To get on track, you must first lay some tracks in the direction of your goals. The "train" of your life runs where you place the tracks. Essentially, you are betting on yourself as you lay those tracks. When you recognize that you are responsible, you can move ahead with focus and energy. B.C. Forbes reinforced personal responsibility with these words:

> Your success depends on you.
>
> You have to steer your own course.
>
> You have to do your own thinking.
>
> You must make your own decisions.
>
> You have to solve your own problems.
>
> Your character is your handiwork.
>
> You have to write your own record.
>
> You have to build your own monument—or dig your own pit.
>
> Which are you doing?

Another Monday Is Coming

Monday is the true test of your feelings about your situation. Do you welcome Monday or dread it? Do you say, "Thank God, it's Friday," or "Thank God, it's Monday?" Do you feel tense and uneasy on Sunday evenings when you think of facing another Monday? When the alarm sounds on Monday, are you painfully aware you still haven't acted on your frustration or desire as you resolved you would? Are you allowing week-after-week of your *one* life to pass without a decision to change? Years ago, a speaker used the following analogy to illustrate this dilemma. He said that indecision is similar to hanging over the center ring of the circus, with one hand on the trapeze swinging forward and your other hand on the trapeze swinging backward. You can't move in either direction until you decide to release the past and swing forward, or release the forward handle and return to the safety of the past. Are you "hanging" over some decisions? Release the handle keeping you in the past and start moving again.

How many more Mondays are you going to dread awakening because you're still stuck in place with no plans for change? Are you using TV or other distractions to avoid thinking about your frustration? Unfortunately, avoidance only postpones the problem. Is your problem or pain just enough to frustrate you but not enough to make you change? Are you expending so much time and energy complaining that you're wasting the energy you could use to find a solution? I've seen individuals use so much energy complaining that they were then too tired to address the existing problem. I've heard some say, "Well, I've thought about this problem enough for one day." Regrettably, this approach doesn't solve the problem, and prolonged, painful indecision is a pass through hell until the person makes a decision.

Your personal freedom and power are attained and maintained through your choices. Power is your ability to take action. Based on your choices to this point, how free and powerful do you feel? You are where you choose to be, but is it where you want to be? If it's not, choose your way out. You have that power, but, like electricity, it's not useful until you choose to turn it on.

Are you already harboring some regrets at your age? Hopefully, you're not, because it's distressing to see people reminiscing about what could have been. Now is your chance to build those memories for later. Are you making choices to create pleasant memories? When your obituary is printed, it will reveal whether you acted on your dreams and frustrations or not. Between now and then, you still have time to live meaningfully. Are you ready for different choices? Another Monday is coming. Why not choose before next Monday?

You Are Where You Choose to Be

Would it surprise you, if I said you are *exactly* where you want to be? You must want to be where you are because you haven't chosen to be somewhere else. If you can accept this truth, you can view choice in a different light. For instance, why waste your time and energy complaining about your situation when it's your choice? Whether it's your job, marriage, relationship, finances, weight, or whatever, your choices have led you to this very moment in each area. When you're frustrated or unhappy, it's much easier to blame others, bad luck, or fate for your situation. Frustration affects most people at some point. However, if complaining becomes your primary response, it's time to stop being helpless and to address the sources of your frustration. Since your choices could be causing some of your difficulties, you can change them for different outcomes. It's not easy, but others have done it and so can you. *Choice* is so important that Chapter Three will focus on this key tool.

Grab Your Life by the Smooth Handle

You succeeded as the *one* to reach life. To get ahead and to enjoy life more, you need to grab your work and life by the smooth handle. You can make things easier by not getting in your own way with your thinking or behavior. Your future can be what you want it to be if you desire it enough and are willing to pay the price to achieve it. You are closer to your dreams and success than you realize. It's the distance between your ears. Your brain is one of the most exceptional creations in the universe; use it to achieve your goals. The future is exciting if you're controlling the direction of your life.

Chapter Two

Talk Yourself to Success

You are influenced more by your self-talk than by what others say to you. You are constantly talking to yourself, even if you aren't always conscious of all your internal messages. For many people, unfortunately, those messages are predominately negative and can undermine their self-image, confidence, and ambition. Psychologist, Shad Helmstetter, Ph.D., states in his excellent book on self-talk, *What To Say When You Talk To Yourself*: "During the first eighteen years of our lives, if we grew up in fairly average, reasonably positive homes, we were told *No!*, or what we could *not* do, more than *148,000 times*." With that overdose of negative conditioning, it's no wonder that so many individuals develop the habit of negative self-talk.

Control Your Internal Messages

This chapter will focus on understanding and controlling your self-talk so it works for you and not against you. Controlling your internal messages is critical to your happiness and success. You can learn to direct your talk and not just passively react to random thoughts and images passing through your head. Basically, you tell yourself what to think and how to feel. Your internal voice can determine the size of your thinking, the quality of your relationships, what you feel you deserve, and whether you live in a shack or a mansion. Your challenge is to recognize the negative messages and replace them with ones you want to hear. Since the words are all inside your head, you're totally in charge of your internal communications. But, since the negative messages are constant and quick, they can influence you before you realize they're there. You have to be continually alert to catch them before they darken your mood or erode your confidence.

Negative Messages Still Influence You

Unless you had a perfect childhood with mostly positive message from parents, siblings, teachers, or coaches, you probably have some negative mental messages that still influence you. Even if you consider yourself motivated, you may still have periods when you don't understand the source of those negative messages. For example, you can feel confident at the beginning of a new job or when thinking of starting your own business, and then—out of the blue—the doubts flood in.

You can begin a new venture with enthusiasm and convince yourself that you're up to the task. But, before you know it, your confidence suddenly collapses, and you begin to wonder why you were crazy enough to think you could actually do what you planned. It's similar to believing you're walking across a ravine on a solid bridge and then suddenly feeling like you're walking across a limp rope. Usually, your confidence can falter after questions such as; "What makes you think you could do this job, or start a business, or write a book?" You can add your own doubtful questions since your mind might have an unlimited supply of negatives that can "surface" at key decision points.

Successful Individuals Also Have Doubts

If it's any consolation, some of the most successful individuals have had to battle similar doubts. According to Dr. Joan C. Harvey's extensive studies, two out of five—and 70% of high achievers—believe that they are faking their way through life. She explored this widespread phenomenon, the Impostor Phenomenon, in *IF I'M SO SUCCESSFUL, WHY DO I FEEL LIKE A FAKE?* According to Dr. Harvey, "The Imposter Phenomenon is a psychological syndrome or pattern. It is based on intense, secret feelings of fraudulence in the face of success and achievement." So, you are not alone, if you have recurring feelings of inadequacy that reinforce your negative self-talk. Often, the difference in performance in many fields is due to effective control of self-talk. Successful performers have learned to talk back to their internal critics. You can learn to do the same.

Steer Your Thoughts

Think of how you start a typical day. Unless you arise and consciously control your thoughts, you will respond to the thoughts and messages that are circulating when you get up. You're usually not even conscious of these influential messages in the early morning. This passive reaction to thoughts is similar to launching a boat from shore. As you push off, and until you start the motor or begin to paddle, the boat will drift with the prevailing current. Your mind also drifts until you take control and steer it as you wish.

Usually, as you roll out of bed, your messages may indicate that you're sleepy, tired, sore, uneasy, or it's too early and you're reluctant to get up. Your "boat" is clearly drifting at that point. When you realize you are mentally drifting, you can regain control with thoughts such as how lucky you are, how well you feel, and how much you're looking forward to the day. You can change your "drift" with self-talk if you really want to. But, half-hearted words or attempts won't change your prevailing moods.

Awareness and Repetition

I don't want to oversimplify the process, but you need to be aware of the messages you receive, and you need to forcefully repeat the messages you want to influence you. Repetition is your paddle or motor. If you repeat "I can do…" (whatever you want to do) with emotion and enthusiasm until it becomes second nature, you'll notice a significant difference in your commitment to your goal. Create your own messages to counter the negative ones you're receiving.

Tip the Scale in Your Favor

To understand the power of messages, visualize a scale inside your head. This scale has two platforms for balance. One side weighs positive messages and the other weighs negative comments. To overcome any negative imbalance, you can add positive self-talk as you would weights. With each repetition of a self-supporting statement, you tip the scale more in your favor. With an unrelenting commitment to feed yourself positive statements, you can overcome negative conditioning. It takes work until it becomes habitual. But, if you're determined to control your thinking, you can do it.

Control Your Internal Critical Parent

Not all negative messages are bad, however. Some express legitimate caution intended to protect you. You have to determine which are helpful and which are limiting. Many of the messages have the tone of a "critical" parent, and they can leave you feeling guilty and unworthy. If you don't believe in child abuse, then don't abuse the child in you with your internal criticism. Your critical parent is at work when you tell yourself that you should have done something, you must do something, or you should not have acted in a certain manner. For example, have you wrestled with a decision to study or work on business at home versus watching TV? What's the source of that voice that makes you feel guilty if you "play?" Learn to treat yourself with the same respect that you give your friends and associates.

You have to remind yourself that *you* make your rules, and you can control that internal voice and give yourself permission to relax and enjoy an evening. For instance, one night I was trying to decide between working on business at home or watching TV. I told myself that I needed a break and had "permission" to watch television. I felt immediate relief as though some parent had just said OK. I thoroughly enjoyed the evening and had no feelings of guilt. You can control your internal parent. It works. Give yourself permission to reduce any overload of self-induced pressure and guilt.

Combine Self-talk with Visualization

You strengthen your motivation when you combine self-talk with visualization of your goals or desired behaviors. You can become enthusiastic by frequently repeating your statement of intention while visualizing your goal. Visualization helps make your goal seem real and achievable. It also helps if you post your written messages where you can see them during the day—in your office, car, or home—and repeat them as you work or drive. Over time, they will penetrate your subconscious and improve your positive outlook.

For the next week, concentrate on listening to your random internal messages. Write them down and notice how many are negative. Then, write out the positive statements that you'll use to reinforce your goals.

Since the negative thoughts are fast and slippery, you'll have to be alert to catch them. You'll be tempted to scratch your head at the origin of many of these negative messages. Since you didn't consciously seek them, where did they originate? They are part of your past conditioning, and if you drop your guard, they will control your thoughts and moods whenever they have a chance. Although, the negative messages are part of your past, they can be controlled with awareness, attention, discipline, and effort, and you can consciously replace them with positive thoughts.

Self-talk is a habit. You can change it by controlling your seemingly "automatic" thoughts. Take control of those thoughts because, as Earl Nightingale wrote, " We become what we think about." Treat your thoughts as sails, and you can harness them to take you anywhere you want to go. Spend the time and effort to change your self-talk and your results will be worth it. You really are worthy. You are authentic and not an impostor. Think positive and talk yourself "up."

Chapter Three

Choice: Your Personal Power

Choice is your personal power. It's your key to many locks along your way. Some decisions lock you in situations you don't like while others bar you from satisfaction and success. Your choices have led to your current situation. If you're not pleased with the results of those choices, you can decide to get better results. Once you understand this liberating reality, you stop feeling like a helpless victim of fate. Instead, you can decide to build the future you want. Quality choices can lead to a better future. Choices are always available, but they are useless if you don't exercise them. Use your power to choose; it can set you free—free to seek or avoid.

Unfortunately, some fearful individuals who haven't learned about choice mentally imprison themselves with irrational, self-imposed restrictions. Once they believe they *can't* do something, that limiting word becomes as strong as any steel prison door. Although victims believe they can't, victors believe they can. Notice how similarly the words *vict or* and *vict im* are spelled. Choice makes the difference.

Your Life Is the Sum of Your Choices

Your life is the sum of your choices, and your decisions have led you to this exact moment. They can also lead you to a brighter future. Why? Because, even if you cannot always control what happens to you, you can control your reaction to others or events and then choose accordingly. The choices that you make today will be your realities tomorrow. You can choose happiness over misery; they are both optional and it's your call. Although you will experience some pain and disappointment as part of life, you can still choose to remain positive. Life is too important for you to feel miserable and unfulfilled.

Start Making Better Choices Now

Even if you're relatively happy now, you can still improve the quality of your choices. In fact, you're ahead of the game if you don't wait for a crisis before making some key choices. To avoid regrets later, do what you need to do now. Make those choices that are the most difficult for you, and they can provide the greatest sense of freedom and release, once you're over your pain or anger. Experience life as you go and don't always wait until you can "afford" what you want. This is not meant to encourage living beyond your means, but you can usually find a way to take your dream cruise, for example. I've seen individuals postpone travel until they retired, and then they died in the first year. Find a way to do what you desire, because by the time you think you can afford it, you can't go back and "buy" those memories you let pass. Sometimes, you need to eat your dessert first because your life is rapidly consuming your future, as it becomes your past.

Life Forces Constant Choices

Life is constantly moving, and it requires choices among the many alternatives you face. Imagine traveling down a road with forks every few yards, and that you are required to make decisions at every juncture. Your decisions at these forks determine the quality of your life. Even if you make some wrong turns, you can recover and choose a better way. Also, when you choose, there's rarely a perfect choice, just a better choice. Your willingness to support the one you choose is what makes it the best one for you. You cannot avoid choice. Even if you don't choose, avoidance becomes your choice by default. The future is coming whether you do something or nothing. Your indecision or inaction won't slow it. Don't decide by default, when you can choose your course.

Success Is Based on Cans

Successful people believe they *can*. Even the spelling of *Amer I can* includes this key phrase of freedom and opportunity. However, many people use the helpless, negative phrase, "I can't," as though it were a physical barrier. They don't realize they are erecting these "can't" barriers in their own minds. Their negative thoughts are like cement blocks that are stacked higher with each use of *can't*. Eventually, enough of the "mental" blocks can wall-off future opportunities for the negative person. The word *can't* is generally nothing more than a self-induced, imaginary limitation; it exists only in the mind of the person who accepts it as reality. While someone might really believe, "I can't" achieve or change, the reality is, "I don't" choose better options.

Successful People Don't Wait for the Right Time

Do you realize how much you can control your life, if you choose to do so? If your personal or work situation is unsatisfactory, you can choose to improve your situation now. If you observe successful people, you'll notice that they don't wait until they feel like working, until conditions are perfect, or until they have more time. In fact, there is no more time. You already have the entire twenty-four hours, and they pass whether you use them or not. No one else has more time than you do. Your challenge is to *focus* your time and effort to accomplish your goals.

Focus until You Finish

It's a challenge to stay focused. Distractions and excuses are all around us. We need the discipline to remain focused until we complete the task at hand. Starting a project is much easier than completing it. A frustrated fellow executive once said, "Find me some finishers; I've got more than enough starters." He had observed too many people getting bogged down or giving up when the work was tough or tedious. Successful individuals realize that many dreams start as drudgery (studying, preparing, training, rewriting, exercising, dieting, sacrificing, financing, etc.). Despite the drudgery, they work through the tempting-to-quit period and finish. When the going gets rough, the will to persist is what separates those who finish from those who don't.

Pull Yourself to Your Goal

If your goal is powerful enough and your discipline is strong enough, you can work your way through the drudgery and frustration between you and your goal. Your real test is to stay focused and committed when you're tired, fired, discouraged, sick, injured, disabled, divorced, overweight, or broke. Strong discipline and willpower are required to keep going when the burdens are heavy and the goals are distant. Hannah More stated a basic truth about this frustrating, testing period when she observed: "Obstacles are those frightful things you see when you take your eyes off the goal." If your goals are clear, the rough spots will pass. However, if your goals are fuzzy, you can start to spot plenty of obstacles.

Remember the following example of the power of goals to get you through the swamp of frustration and drudgery. Imagine you're in a truck and stuck in the muck of the swamp. You have a winch and cable on the front bumper. You pick out a tree on the other side, and you unroll the cable and attach it to that tree. As you apply power to the winch, it pulls you to the tree and to dry ground. That tree and cable represent the pulling-power of your goals to get you through your swamp of frustration. Clear goals can draw you toward them. Use your mental winch to pull you to your goals. This technique works.

Completed Work Has Value

You can only graduate, get promoted, achieve, or build your reputation with completed work. Your reputation is based on what you've actually done, not on what you could do or plan to do. Talk is cheap, but successful completion has value. Anyone can talk about what they could do, but they eat the dust of those who actually accomplish their plans. Don't just say you could do it; don't just try. Do it.

You can always find the time to do those things you want to do. Likewise, you have an amazing reserve of energy for those activities and projects that you like. With discipline and practice, you can learn to "Do it now" and not allow your likes or dislikes to affect your work. Refuse to allow yourself excuses for procrastination or weak performance, and you'll be well on the way to more success.

Your Life's Meter Is Running: Start Now

The phrase, "Use it or lose it," absolutely applies to time. If you don't believe it, try to relive the past hour or yesterday. Unfortunately, they are now memories. Your future can be what you decide it will be, but you have to start it. You might even have to jump-start it, if you've been procrastinating. It sounds obvious, but you cannot do what you want to do until you start. Why not get off your "but" excuse and start now? Your friends, relatives, and associates tire of hearing you complain about your frustrations if they don't see you working to resolve them. Are you making excuses for not starting? Instead of making excuses, convert your frustration into action that will meet your needs.

Your Answers Are Within You

During your quiet moments, if you hear your inner voice reminding you there's more to life than this, you are probably facing some decisions that your mind and body know intuitively you need to make. The answers you need are within you. Listen to your own guidance. If you can't hear yourself above the crowd around you, then you need some time alone. You require time and courage to explore your inner needs.

However, I've known individuals who were reluctant to hear what their inner voices might reveal. Some were locked into economically satisfying lifestyles, and, even if they hated their jobs or their work environments, they still wouldn't face the prospect of change. Others couldn't change because they were living a role (doctor, lawyer, engineer, accountant, etc.) to satisfy a parent or loved one. Despite being miserable, they lacked the will to change.

Although self-knowledge is important, there are some risks with introspection. You can be reminded of some inner truths that you might already know, but that you can't afford to acknowledge. These truths might conflict with your marriage, relationship, career, profession, or compensation. For example, you could agonize over continuing in your field or profession or becoming a schoolteacher, social worker, or a minister. Further, you could wrestle with the urge to leave a successful career to coach, join the Peace Corps, enter public service, or go back to school. Although introspection is risky, it can lead to significant changes in your life.

But, if you don't listen to yourself, you can continue down the wrong road for you. Also, if you suppress your inner voice long enough, you can risk mental illness. I've known some individuals who eventually collapsed under the pressure of a career they detested. They wouldn't leave on their own, and their emotions finally forced it for them. Fortunately, they recovered after an extended period, and they found their niches in new careers. So, don't ignore your inner nudges and messages. It's healthier and wiser to listen to your best friend...you.

Some Key Choices that Determine the Quality of Your Life

The following choices might be similar to some you're currently facing. As you will see throughout this book, you do have choices. Use the power of choice to improve your chances for success and satisfaction. You can choose to:

- Maintain good health or let yourself "go" physically.
- Lose weight and gain confidence or remain overweight and lack confidence.
- Plan your life or allow someone else to control it for you.
- Ask for what you want or hope someone will eventually read your mind.

- Make things happen in your life or merely accept whatever happens to you.
- Go after what you want or passively watch your dreams fade away.
- Use difficulties to prove yourself or view your problems as burdens to bear.
- Realize you are more fortunate than most or feel sorry for yourself.
- Get mad and trigger your survival instincts or feel and act like a helpless victim.
- Reverse a poor choice or remain in a bad job, relationship, or marriage because you're too proud or too stubborn to admit it isn't working.
- Become financially secure or remain financially stressed with excessive debt.
- Change a bad situation or endure the frustrating consequences of not changing.
- Work harder to prove you're worth more or just complain about your job and pay.
- Seek a position that rewards your contribution or stay frustrated where you are.
- Shoulder your own responsibility or blame your troubles on fate or someone else.
- Seek a healthier, positive environment or associate with negative, cynical people.
- Continue to learn or hope your current knowledge will carry you to retirement.
- Pull out of your rut and stay out or remain in a boring, comfortable rut for life.
- Get what you like or be forced to like what you get in work or life.
- Think big, think success or feel grateful that you even have a job.

- Aim and control your one-and-only life or regretfully watch the years slip away.
- Believe it's never too late to still achieve or live and die with your unrealized potential.
- Control your thoughts and attitude or reflect the thoughts and attitudes around you.
- Love and respect yourself or be at the mercy of the world's opinion of you.

These are some of the choices that will determine the quality of your future. You can change your life by changing your choices. Many lives have been changed with better choices. The process is neither rocket science nor magic. You can start where you are right now.

Although Invisible, the Choices Are There

Wherever you're sitting at this moment, you are surrounded by invisible radio waves that you can receive by simply turning on a radio. Music, news, sports, and weather are as close as the touch of a button. As you sit there, you are also surrounded by invisible choices. In a moment of frustration, anger, guilt, pain, desperation, hope or inspiration, you can reach for one of those decisions that can free you and renew you. You can change by deciding, "I've had it and I will change," or "I want it and I will get it." These choices are available twenty-four hours each day if you are aware of and receptive to them.

These invisible choices, like the streets of your city, are there whether you use them or not. If you have transportation and a map, you can go anywhere you wish. The same is true with choices. Choices are the roads to get you there, but you must provide the mental map of directions. If you don't know what you want or where you want to go, choices can't help. Choices are valuable if you are decisive but they are wasted if you're not. When you have options, you have personal freedom because options can keep you from feeling helpless. However, your options are only valuable and real if you choose among them; otherwise, they're just illusions. It's worth your time and effort to think about the many choices still available to you at this stage. Your choices distinguish you from every other person on earth. Distinguish yourself with your decisions.

Remember that in spite of all the advice and counsel you receive, it's your game and your life. Your life is your main event. Manage it well and you can create those great memories for later years. If your current memories are not the ones you want to remember, then grab one of those invisible decisions and start changing now. Don't wait for fate to intervene on your behalf or delay because you erroneously believe that somcone will come to rescue you from your personal responsibility. Don't put it off any longer. Use your personal power to change. Remind yourself that "If it's to be, it's up to me." Do it now.

Chapter Four

Attitude Is Key

A positive, winning attitude is a major asset. You control your attitude and determine if it's positive or negative. Your control starts as you arise and dress. While bathing or dressing, you are already choosing the thoughts that shape your attitude for the day. You "put on" your attitude with your clothing every day. Each day is neutral, and your attitude can influence whether you have a good or bad day. Your attitude can pave your way or block your way. Also, you project your energy and spirit, and others can quickly recognize your attitude by your facial expression, body language, and the tone of your voice. They only need a few seconds to determine your mood. They can tell if you're happy and positive, or if you act like you have Limburger cheese on your upper lip, and you think the whole world "smells" at the moment.

Your attitude is so influential that it flavors most of what you see, hear, or do. Regarding flavor, the vineyard offers a good example of contrasting tastes. Although champagne and vinegar are both made from grapes, there's an obvious difference in taste. Similarly, success and failure both result from thoughts, but they produce entirely different outcomes. Attitude can influence whether your life is filled with bitter or pleasant tastes.

Some Advantages of Being Positive

Your perspective determines whether you believe your future will be bright or not. Attitude is determined by your thoughts, and you can choose to control those thoughts. Since attitude is a choice, here are some reasons for choosing a positive one:

- You can be happier. A good attitude doesn't guarantee less stress or a problem-free life, but you are better prepared to deal with the difficulties you confront. You can still choose to be happy despite your challenges.
- Others will have more interest in helping you if you are positive and don't dwell on negatives.
- Your work can be easier because you choose it and appreciate the job or profession you have. When you choose your work, you are more likely to enjoy it.
- A positive attitude can improve your chances for promotions, pay increases, bonuses, or other incentives offered by your organization. You are more motivated to go the "extra mile" when you are recognized and rewarded. You can stand out because there's no crowd on the extra mile.
- If you depend on gratuities for a significant portion of your income, your attitude can be the difference between minimum and maximum tips. If you choose to provide a service, do it with enthusiasm. Choose to like what you do and your attitude and extra effort will show. Customers don't want to *pay* to be served by a disgruntled individual. If you're unhappy with your work or management, don't burden the customers with it. Strangers don't want to pay to hear your problems when they can hear them at home or at work for free. You are there by choice. Admittedly, rude, obnoxious patrons or unruly kids can test you, but these customers are part of the job in many cases. If you really don't enjoy dealing

with them, do yourself and them a favor; find another job more suited to your interest, temperament, and personality. Remind yourself that misery is optional.

- A positive attitude can aid your marriage, love life, or other relationship because you aren't bitter or miserable over your current situation. You're a better companion as a result.

- You can address problems more readily. Positive people are action-oriented and don't wait for fate or luck to resolve their problems. Don't wait for the answers; go find them.

- You will have more energy. A positive attitude helps increase your energy while a negative one can exhaust you. A negative friend or associate can also drain you if you aren't careful.

- You can be more optimistic because you see a brighter future for yourself. Positive anticipation can increase your motivation significantly. Always have something positive to move toward and you won't be bored with your life.

- You can choose to be happy where you are. Since you are only as happy as you tell yourself you are, you can be as elated right here and now as you could be anywhere else. For example, you can be miserable on a dream vacation or ecstatic over simple pleasures at home. What you tell yourself is what you feel. Happiness and misery are not external conditions. They are internal thoughts and feelings based on your interpretation of what's outside. Therefore, you're the master of your moods and emotions.

Some Causes of Negative Thinking

If a positive attitude is so important, why do some of your friends, relatives, and associates still maintain negative, cynical, or fearful attitudes? I believe some of the reasons are:

- They were raised in families where negative attitudes were prevalent, and they unconsciously adopted some negative habits during their formative years.
- They weren't taught that they could control their thoughts and didn't understand that they aren't at the mercy of random, fearful thoughts.
- They suffered some early setbacks and concluded that life wasn't fair. They might have lowered their expectations at that point. By not even trying, they passively extinguished those dreams they could have realized with more positive attitudes.
- Some negative individuals believe that people with enthusiasm are phony or political. They confuse being positive with being political. However, in their own case, they don't believe they are cynical or negative. They just see themselves as being *realistic*. Once they believe that, it's difficult to change their distorted view.
- Some fear disappointment. For instance, I knew an individual who believed it was better to be a pessimist and be surprised than to be an optimist and be disappointed. Unfortunately, with this negative belief, he wasn't surprised very often.
- To be positive is to risk. However, some feel that it's easier and safer to be a victim since they can blame others for their condition. They appear to feel it's more comfortable to justify failure or low expectations than try to succeed. Unfortunately, what they rationalize as a trade-off can become a give-up in a key area of their life. An example would be remaining in a "safe" job for security, even though it drains the person's spirit. I've known many of these individuals over the years.
- When they see successful individuals suffer setbacks, they may feel it justifies their cynicism about the futility of trying to get ahead.
- They see themselves as helpless and don't see a way out. Most of them don't believe that the future will be any better than the present.

A psychologist described some of them as "throw-up artists." They throw-up mostly negatives, and if someone tries to help them, they throw-up all the reasons the suggestions won't work for them. They just don't get it.

It can be rewarding or painful to help the negative people you care about. You can try to help them be more positive and control their thoughts and life, but you need to maintain your own positive attitude in the process. Sometimes, your assistance works, but it can be a draining process. It's like trying to save someone caught in a whirlpool. The challenge is to pull them out without being pulled in. Be wary, because their strong negative thoughts and emotions can draw you in.

Ways to Improve Your Attitude

If you want to improve your attitude, here are some ways to consider:

- Concentrate on becoming conscious of each negative thought you create and replace it with a positive one as soon as you catch yourself. Because your thinking is a habit, you need feedback to increase your awareness. To become aware faster, ask a friend or associate to tell you when they observe you being negative. Another awareness technique is to slip a rubber band around your wrist and snap it against your arm each time you catch yourself thinking negatively. With awareness, you can gain more control of your thoughts and attitude.

- Get in the right mood with a daily ritual. Start your self-talk as you awaken and as you bathe or dress. Remind yourself what a great day it is and how well you feel. Create your own positive thoughts to emphasize. Control the start of your day, reinforce it during the day with positive thoughts, and you should notice a difference in your attitude. You know that you need more than one meal per day to maintain your energy. Likewise, you can enhance your attitude with motivational nourishment throughout the day. Don't skimp on nutrition or motivation.

- If you're around negative friends and associates, you can try to help change their attitudes, but if you can't, you might seek some new, positive acquaintances. You become a product of your negative surroundings if you don't manage your environment. Remember that success breeds success. If you associate with successful, positive individuals, you are bound to absorb some of their qualities. Consciously learn from positive models of happiness and success. Negative friends are hard to give up, but with negative associates, you might have to win them over or weed them from your circle, if you want a more positive environment. Cynics don't build anything, but they can undermine your spirit and morale if you stay around them long enough. Your environment is important because your mind accepts a negative message as readily as a positive one. It can't tell the difference between positive and negative and responds to the frequency and emotional intensity of the messages it receives. Your value system knows the difference, but your mind does not. What messages are you receiving in your personal and work environments?

- Elevate your thinking with more reading and less TV. Increase your motivation by visiting the self-help/self-improvement section of your local bookstore or finding self-help books on the Web. You can usually find enough choices to meet your needs for self-development. In addition, there are some excellent audiotapes on additional subjects of interest. Further, in the Appendix, I've listed some books that can help you. Books and tapes can take you to places you haven't been, and they can provide knowledge and experience that you haven't had. These books can provide speedy access to some of the best thinking on your areas of interest. Learn from successful role models by reading their books. You can change habits and limitations with the aid of those authors who provide valuable information, insight, and advice. Self-improvement books and tapes are good sources of mental vitamins. Use tapes to add value to your driving time. Read, listen, and expand your world.

- On a three-by-five card, list some thoughts or habits you want to change. You can also write positive affirmations you want to emphasize and remember. Review the card(s) three or four times a day and before you go to bed. Gradually, the repetition of these thoughts or affirmations will become part of your new thought process. Most of what you currently believe, whether in life or religion, was formed by repetition. Repetition is powerful, and frequent repetition is required to change your thoughts and actions. Benjamin Franklin, among many others, changed his behavior by listing and reviewing the qualities he wanted to acquire or improve. This technique works, if you work at it.

- Ask positive friends and associates how they stay "up." They will probably be glad to share their philosophy and technique for staying motivated. They have faced many of the same challenges you have, and they have managed to remain positive. Unfortunately, less successful people often mistakenly believe that positive achievers have it *easier* than they do. However, in many cases, the upbeat ones have faced as many or more hard times as anyone else. Despite their share of adversity, they've chosen to be positive anyway.

- One key to a better attitude is to be more forgiving of yourself and others. If God can forgive, why are you so hard on yourself and others? Your ego might be keeping you from forgiving. Forgiving yourself can release you from guilt about what you've done or failed to do. Guilt can drain much of your energy if you feel unworthy about aspects of your life. You are probably as normal as anyone else, but you may be judging yourself too harshly in terms of *shoulds* and *oughts*. Just remember that you plan your own guilt trips, and no one else can make you feel guilty without your agreement. By forgiving others, you free yourself from the anger and resentment of judging those around you. Since there is usually little or no positive payoff for you, is it really worth your anger and frustration when you judge and criticize others? If you don't forgive others, you'll spend more time thinking about them than you do about your friends and family. When you refuse to forgive, you only penalize yourself. Forgiveness is similar to weighing anchor before sailing. You can't leave port with your anchor still imbedded below. Where is your anchor at this point? Only you can haul it in and sail on. Forgiveness might be your answer. It's a powerful "release." Forgive...and get on with your life.

- Improve your attitude with an improved spiritual life. Many churches and temples have members and staff that are cheerful, caring, and can offer positive support and counsel. Let others help you lighten your burden, and allow a stronger faith to calm your fears. You can turn to God and the timeless power of prayer to help you through your distress. Also, don't underestimate the energizing power of the group. A single log that falls from the fire goes out much faster than the combined logs remaining. Increase your energy and spirit with the support of the group.

- Look forward with anticipation to more things in your life. When you have positive goals and plans, each day is more meaningful. Keep looking forward with positive expectancy and you won't be glancing backward with regret. Do what you feel you need to do now, and you'll have happier memories later. Don't ever let it be said that your future is *behind* you. If you're looking backward too much, ask yourself why. It might be that you've quit planning for the future. Your remaining future is still important. Concentrate on going forward with enthusiasm and a sense of direction.

- Remember that you are special and your life has meaning. Count your blessings. You are more fortunate than you realize in terms of family, friends, a home, a job, and good health. In some cases, you are more fortunate than some of the people you might envy. Don't assume that everyone else has it "made." You might be surprised by the reality behind some of the masks of happiness and success worn by others. You could discover that some of those you envy, actually envy you. Some individuals will go to great lengths to present a façade of success, happiness, and even sanity. Then a scandal, divorce, suicide, or other traumatic event reveals the truth behind the image. So, don't count someone else's money or take his or her happiness or state of mind for granted. Appearances can be deceiving. You could be mistaken in your assumptions about their confidence, happiness, success, or net worth, while putting yourself down and devaluing your own assets and favorable circumstances.

You will probably experience some difficult periods in your life, and your attitude can be a life preserver during those turbulent times. Even if it appears that nothing is working in your life at this point, a positive attitude can help sustain you until your situation changes, and it will. I can't emphasize too strongly how much you can control your attitude, and that it is one of your most important tools for a successful life. Allow yourself no latitude on attitude. As all sailors know, you cannot control the wind, but you can adjust your sails to reach any destination in the world. You sail with your attitude. Is your attitude helping you stay on course at this stage of life?

Chapter Five

Growing from Adversity

Unless you're the exception, you've experienced some adversity along the way. Your problems could have involved setbacks, losses, pains, or disappointments from unexpected misfortunes. Despite your temporary frustration, pain, or anger, adversity can advance your personal growth, if you can see beyond the loss to lessons from the experience. Sometimes, tears are the best corrective lenses for improved vision following a setback. When hardships or reverses occur, you can adjust more readily by learning to cope effectively. As you cope, you grow.

If you can't sleep and find yourself staring at the ceiling while agonizing over your situation, you can feel lonely, confused, helpless, and scared. However, you are not alone in facing personal misfortunes, and you can learn to cope with your problems. Coping is more productive than moping about the misfortune or merely hoping your situation will improve.

Unfortunately, you might not have been taught effective coping skills or trained to look for the opportunity in adversity. This chapter includes some techniques to help you cope more effectively.

Strength from Adversity

Surprisingly, during adversity when you're more vulnerable, you can actually grow more than when you're successful. Some of the ways you can grow are to:

- Bounce back stronger when you're knocked to your knees. You can discover or rediscover your religious beliefs and bolster your spiritual needs.
- Learn that failure is a meaningless label, and that setbacks are opportunities for learning, growing, and starting anew.
- Discover that you have value, which is independent of your work or family roles.
- Seek psychological or career counseling to help you get back on track.
- End a bad relationship and go in a new direction. Find more happiness and success with a new a new partner. Sometimes, adversity is the final straw in a relationship that has no chance of working. Leaving is painful, and it takes courage, but this process has changed many lives for the better. You know when the relationship is limiting or damaging to you and the other person. You know when it's time.
- Learn new skills and seek new opportunities. There are opportunities that you don't know about yet. Information and contacts can open your eyes to new possibilities.
- Strengthen your willpower and discipline during adverse periods.
- Become mentally tougher and draw on inner reserves of strength.
- Tap your resourceful imagination for ideas on dealing with the setback.
- Learn to control your self-talk to resolve, and not aggravate, the current problem.
- Take the opportunity to pause, appreciate life, and enjoy the present moment with your family, friends, and pet(s).

- Learn to count your blessings and not just focus on what you might have lost or missed due to some adversity. Count them daily as motivational refreshment.

The more you are tested, the more you advance or retreat. Tough times can definitely make you or break you. Let your difficulties "make" you, as you learn and grow from the experience.

Bounce Back Stronger

With success, you may pause and give thanks for your good fortune, but you might not examine why you succeeded or what you learned along the way. When you're "full of yourself," you can be blind to your faults or to the lessons that even achievement can teach. When your life is going great, it's easy to believe that you're the center of the universe. Your ego can be a great asset in boosting your confidence, but it can trip you if it becomes overinflated.

If you experience setbacks, they can force a level of introspection that moments of glory do not. Disappointments can teach you more than success if you're open to the painful lessons. For instance, if you suffer the loss of your job, marriage, relationship, confidence, or self-esteem, your grief can trigger reflections and resolutions about changes that you need to make.

Whether you feel positive or negative depends on your attitude about the adversity at hand. If you're resilient, you deal with what's happened, regardless of how frustrated or hurt you feel. Learn from the difficulty and look beyond the current disappointment. Since you usually learn good judgment from bad judgment, each adversity can advance your growth. Only you can decide if you're going to be better or bitter as a result of the experience.

Some Ways to Grow through Coping

If you're experiencing personal problems as you read this book, the following suggestions may help you work through them:

- Force yourself to rest. Stress and pressure can disrupt your sleep, distort your perspective, and cause you to feel overwhelmed by your situation. As Coach Vince Lombardi stated, "Fatigue makes a coward of us all." Fear and paranoia can grow rapidly in the fertile field of your fatigue. Also, you water your fear and paranoia with your thoughts, and there's much more water when you're exhausted. But, when you're rested, your problems become more manageable.

- Keep telling yourself that you'll get through this period, even if you don't yet know how. Your difficulty has a limited time frame and it will pass. Your longest, worst hour still has only sixty minutes. You've handled tough situations before. See yourself on the other side of this one and visualize how it will look in two or three years. Your life will go on. Dr. Robert H. Schuller wrote a book with a title appropriate to your situation: *Tough Times Never Last, But Tough People Do!*

- Take some quiet time and list each issue bothering you. When you're in the midst of events, it's easy to lose your perspective. You can become so confused that your thoughts seem like tangled spaghetti in a bowl, and you can't tell where one piece ends and another begins. When you're confused and your thoughts are running wild, you might feel like a rancher trying to inventory the herd during a stampede. But, when you take a break and list your concerns, you can separate the serious from the routine and deal with them in their order of importance. Getting your issues on paper clears the mental cobwebs, eases your tension, and clarifies your thinking. Otherwise, the jumble of ideas, thoughts, emotions, and fears can confuse and overwhelm you. If you don't itemize and separate your concerns, you can feel threatened by the size of the problem. Cut your problem down to size with your list. This process works.

- To rekindle your spirits, vividly recall a period when you felt strong and proud. Perhaps, you won a contest, received an award, or were recognized for some achievement. Visualize your proudest moment and recreate those emotions you felt at that time. Concentrate on that image with its sights, sounds, and surroundings until you actually feel as you did then. Put yourself in your own winner's circle by recalling how good you are. To win, you have to feel like a winner. Positive recall helps if you take the time to experience it.

- In addition to the stress of your current situation, you can further upset your mental and emotional balance with poor nutrition or lack of exercise. Good nutrition can make a major difference in your energy, alertness, imagination, and attitude. For exercise, even short walks can boost your spirit or change your perspective. With improved nutrition and exercise, you can see the world through different eyes. I've experienced the significant difference that exercise, good meals, and vitamins have made in my moods and outlook. Therefore, I believe that if your thinking is fuzzy or you feel edgy and tired, the cause might not be just your situation or job; you could need a balanced diet and some exercise. You can become so tired or so nutritionally deprived, that fatigue, headaches, paranoia, and irritability seem normal. It's scary when you believe that's the way you're supposed to feel each day. Depending on your schedule and lifestyle, fatigue can develop so gradually that it almost seems normal. Wake up! You don't have to feel so shaky, irritable, or tired. You control the power to change your energy level. Provide enough fuel for your mind and body so they can help you handle your challenges. Tough times demand your best thinking and emotional equilibrium. What you eat does affect how you think and feel.

- Get a physical examination. What you are feeling might be due to some undiagnosed illness or condition. Also, if you suspect something is wrong, why put off finding out? You can get help if there is a problem or get relief if there's not. Arrange to be examined and tested. Life is too short to be impaired by a physical condition that can be healed or repaired. Today, much pain and suffering can be relieved with modern medical techniques. Why wait and worry? Get the facts about your actual condition.

- Strengthen your spiritual life by attending religious services. Many have found peace and solace with a stronger faith and the support of congregation members. A live service with the uplifting power of fellowship with like-minded people can boost your spirits. The doors are open and you can start at any time. If you're harboring a grudge over a negative religious experience in the past, don't take it to the grave with you. You only hurt yourself if you don't forgive and forget the past. You can still live with joy and love, but you've got to open your heart and mind to do it.

- More people are turning to the Internet as a source for connecting with support groups. There are groups for many specific types of issues or concerns. It can be therapeutic to know that others are experiencing similar feelings.

- Get a copy of *A Course in Miracles* or one of the numerous books related to it. There are also various tapes available. One of the books is *Love Is Letting Go of Fear* by Gerald G. Jampolsky, M.D. Dr. Jampolsky and many others have credited *A Course in Miracles* with helping turn their lives around. If you want to experience more love and happiness and less fear and guilt, these books can help. Open yourself to new ways of seeing.

- You've heard it before, but if you count your blessings daily, you are reminded of the good things in your life. It's easy to take blessings for granted if you don't recall them frequently. Practice your attitude of gratitude daily and you'll develop a more positive outlook.

- Lighten your burden by offering support to others with situations worse than yours. By offering support and encouragement, you raise your spirits by focusing on someone other than yourself. As Dr. Jampolsky states in his book, "Love is the total absence of fear." As a result, you cannot love and fear at the same time. Consider the wisdom of love versus fear and strive for more love in your life. You can be happier and less fearful.

- Try to maintain a sense of humor despite your problems. Find something to smile about and learn to see the humorous side of people or events. Associate with positive, cheerful people, and they can help boost your spirits. Laughter really is good for the spirit when it reminds you that you might be taking yourself or life too seriously.

- If you haven't found relief by this point, find someone who can help with the answer. You can seek answers from a family member, friend, associate, minister, rabbi, priest, or a professional therapist. Ask for help. It doesn't pay to be timid, reluctant, stubborn, or too proud to ask, when you desperately need a helping hand.

The prior list of suggestions may help with your current situation. The next section covers some approaches for coping with future issues or dealing with some repetitive situations that bother you. The following section also includes some thoughts on changing your "perceptions" to avoid unnecessary difficulties.

Cope by Controlling Your Reaction

Although you cannot always control what happens to you, you can control your reaction. If no death or serious injury is involved, most occurrences are neutral until you decide how you will react. You choose the degree of emotional intensity you invest in each situation. Your choices can range from feelings that "It's no problem" to "It's a catastrophe."

For example, consider your reaction to the other drivers during rush hour traffic. The drivers that cut you off or honk impatiently are just anonymous, impersonal individuals until you label them and react accordingly. You can choose to feel highly offended and angry (How could those drivers do that to me?), or you can choose to feel no hostility and allow the other drivers equal use of the road. Similar choices apply to your reaction to the weather, disappointment, your job, your boss, a loved one, or any other person or situation. Remember that the other drivers' horns or others' words are not direct-wired to your "hot" button. There's a delay between their stimulus and your response, and that key space is reserved for the reaction you *choose*. What you might think is an automatic response to stimulus is actually a response you choose. It just happens so fast, you don't realize that your thoughts actually precede your reaction.

Control your reactions to others and events by controlling your self-talk. You see what you tell yourself to see and feel what you tell yourself to feel. For example, if you have a great day one day and a lousy one the next, the primary difference is your internal dialogue. The world doesn't change overnight, but your self-talk does, if you don't manage it. Become aware of your self-talk and you can control it. Don't allow negative self-talk to control your moods.

Cope by Getting Mad versus Being Sad

After an appropriate period of grief following some misfortune, you might need to quit feeling sorry for yourself and get mad. Some sadness is normal following a loss, but excessive or extended sadness won't activate your fighting spirit or trigger your survival instincts. If you continue to feel sad beyond any reasonable period of grief, you only dig a deeper emotional hole for yourself. Sadness can cause you to feel helpless as long as you're in that emotional state. However, when you're angry, you can regain your winning spirit, resolve to bounce back, and decide to act.

This type of anger can be productive and healthy versus an immature, unproductive tendency to blow-up. Sometimes it's OK for you to be unreasonable and to refuse to accept a lame excuse or *no* for an answer. People who become "selectively" unreasonable can often get results that sad or submissive individuals cannot. Although someone noted that *anger* is only one letter short of *danger*, don't be afraid to get mad when appropriate. It's a good catharsis following sadness. When you're indignant, you have a burning desire to prove you'll overcome your temporary hardship.

Cope by Correcting Your Perception

You can make your adversity even worse if you distort your perception of what has actually happened. You can misperceive because you see things through the filtered mental glasses you wear. For example, how many times have you seen two individuals experience the same situation but react in completely opposite ways? The view of the glass as half-full or half-empty illustrates this perceptual bias. You don't see things as they are, but as you are. Like beauty, the perception of reality is in your eye. Under the stress of adversity, you can materially distort the reality you think you see. Keep this in mind as you read the following.

In terms of perception, neither your nor my mind can distinguish between what we imagine and what we actually experience. Our minds cannot determine if the signal or image originated outside or from another part of the brain. Top athletes have learned that visualizing successful performance can be as effective as actually practicing the same skill for limited periods. The mind and muscles record the details of the visualized action the same as actual experience. This process allows an individual to mentally rehearse performance. If you want to improve, see it in your mind first. What you see, really can be.

We Can Distort what We Think Is Real

Also, you and I are far more vulnerable to the power of suggestion than we might believe. I discovered this while working with hypnosis in high school and college. As an amateur hypnotist, I was amazed to learn about the power of suggestion and how we can distort what we think is real.

For example, if I put you to sleep and ask you to open your eyes and look at a wall, I could suggest that you see a door in the middle of a solid wall, and you would see the door I described. Conversely, I could remove an actual door from a wall by suggesting that you don't see it. Even if I mentioned you could see a pink elephant on the table, you would clearly see the elephant, and in living color. How could this happen? As a teenager, I was curious about the process that could create an image that didn't exist and remove an image that was real. Prior to my experience with hypnosis, I thought that what I saw was real. After that, I realized that my eyes were not always fixed on what was actually there.

In attempting to understand the phenomenon of "selective" vision, I concluded that we have a mental slide projector or video camera, and that we project distortions of what we think we see. We can project our hopes, fears, shortcomings, and self-images. For instance, what we see in the mirror is not necessarily what others see when they look at us. Our visual distortions can vary from minor differences to major discrepancies.

The Power of Self-Image

For example, plastic surgeons discovered that some patients, despite seeking an attractive new face, still saw the old self-image when the bandages were removed. Despite flawless cosmetic surgery, the surgeon's knife couldn't alter the self-image behind the face. The old image was still projected from the reservoir of negative, self-image slides. This pattern became common enough following successful surgeries that Dr. Maxwell Maltz, a famous plastic surgeon, developed an interest in the controlling power of the self-image. He wrote about this subject in his highly acclaimed bestseller, *Psycho-Cybernetics*. If patients who volunteered for elective surgery cannot see the positive changes in their own faces, then you can appreciate the power and influence of selective vision among the general population. Be conscious of this tendency in yourself because what you see, might not be real.

Cope with the Power of Suggestion

I referred earlier to the power of suggestion. Suggestions from inside us and from others are so powerful that we don't have to be hypnotized for them to influence us. For example, when I would try to hypnotize some individuals, I couldn't put them to sleep. However, they were so vulnerable to suggestion that I could still control some of their actions even while they were awake.

One of my high school friends clearly fit this category, and he and I learned how impressionable he was one afternoon while we were shooting basketball in the backyard. I told him that he could do everything but shoot the ball. Naturally, he laughed and dribbled toward the goal to prove me wrong. Just as he started to shoot, his arms locked in place and he couldn't release the ball. He remained frozen in position until I told him he could shoot.

We were both amazed and amused by this. As a further test, I told him he could shoot, but he couldn't move his right foot. Again, he didn't believe it, but when he tried to move, he couldn't lift his foot. His foot was totally immobilized until I told him he could move it. After these two examples, he was a true believer. Even though he was bright, wide-awake, and knew my instructions limiting his movements were ridiculous, he couldn't consciously ignore my command.

What's your situation? Are you allowing your internal voice or someone else's advice, counsel, or opinion to freeze your beliefs, thoughts, or actions? Based on the potential impact of suggestions on you, it's imperative that you recognize the stopping-power of the word *can't* or other self-limiting words or images that you either repeat to yourself or accept from others. Your distorted thinking can cause you to believe something that just isn't so. Whatever you see in your mind is what will be. It's your choice whether it's positive and successful or negative and painful. Why not create those mental slides and videos that portray you as capable and successful? After all, you are the director of your life.

Cope with the Power of Patience and Persistence

When we are frustrated or hurt, patience and persistence can be powerful allies in getting through those periods. Sometimes, life ambushes our best-laid plans. While planning for the future, we can be blind-sided by the unexpected. Even when we feel we're on the right road, some of us have learned that success and happiness don't always travel in straight lines. Despite our best plans and efforts, we may experience flat tires, potholes, detours, or dead-ends on the way to our goals. Often, we have to back up, regroup, and find a new approach. Also, there are times when it seems we were selected for special hardships because two or three misfortunes occur close together. These periods of back-to-back problems probably gave rise to the saying, "Without bad luck, I'd have no luck at all." When we're feeling down and wondering how much more we can take, it's critical that we don't give up and quit trying.

Cope by Never Giving Up

Effective individuals refuse to give up. Many have succeeded through sheer staying power. Winston Churchill epitomized this spirit as he rallied the British people during World War II. The ability to bounce back and keep going is critical to eventual success. One boxer said that the key to winning a fight was to get off the canvas, even when you thought you couldn't get up. Those who refused to stay down have won many fights in the ring and in life. Many champions managed to keep fighting "just one more round" until they won.

Coach Lombardi and others in many different fields have stressed the importance of making a "second effort." Often, when you try *one more time*, you succeed. Unfortunately, too many people quit trying after being rebuffed or turned down the first time. Although a second effort can be effective, Chuck Reaves took this concept even further in his book, *THE THEORY OF 21*. He wrote: "For every person who will say yes, there are twenty who will say no. For a positive response you must find the twenty-first person." So, when you're tempted to give up, don't quit until you've tried the twenty-first person. Believe that your idea or plan is worth this extra effort.

During the gold rush in California, some discouraged miners gave up after months or years of hard work and sacrifice. Other miners followed the quitters, and, occasionally, they discovered gold near the previous miner's last dig. When you're tempted to quit, remind yourself that you might be doing the right things but the results just aren't there yet. While waiting for better results, you can become temporarily discouraged until you regain control of your attitude and spirit.

If you're tempted to give up, remember this frequently used motivational phrase, and it might help pull you through: "Winners don't quit, and quitters don't win." Another helpful statement that has remained true over many years is: "Where there's a will, there's a way."

Persistence has been a key for many people, and it helped Ray Kroc build McDonald's into a household name. The following was his credo since he founded McDonald's:

PRESS ON

Nothing in the world can take the place of persistence.

Talent will not; nothing is more common than unsuccessful
men with talent.

Genius will not; unrewarded genius is almost a proverb.

Education alone will not; the world is full of educated
derelicts.

Persistence and determination alone are omnipotent.

Persistence was also a major factor in the following situation: "This was to be our final season in The Valley. Six full seasons we had excavated there, and season after season had drawn a blank; we had worked for months at a stretch and found nothing, and only an excavator knows how desperately depressing that can be; we had almost made up our minds that we were beaten, and were preparing to leave The Valley and try our luck elsewhere; and then…hardly had we set hoe to ground in our last despairing effort than we made a discovery that exceeded our wildest dreams." These were Howard Carter's words in the winter of 1922, upon discovering King Tut's Tomb.

So, the next time you eat at McDonald's, see King Tut's exhibit at the museum, or read about his tomb, remember that unrelenting persistence was the key to success. Persistence can also be your key. So, recall these examples when you get discouraged and don't even think about giving up on your challenge or opportunity. Press on!

Cope by Understanding Timing and Conditions

Sometimes the breakthrough or answer is related to timing or conditions. I learned this from observing gardeners and farmers in the rural area where I grew up. In my small school, each male student was required to take F.F.A., Future Farmers of America, and we were taught the importance of climate and conditions for growth. The farmers worked in harmony with the seasons and cycles to enhance the growth of their crops and plants. They knew that fruits and vegetables only grow during certain seasons and under specific conditions.

Similar to plants, perhaps your plan or idea is facing a season or conditions obstacle. In some cases you may just need more time and patience to realize your goal. Sometimes, you can't force the future or conditions, no matter how great your idea is at the moment. Often, you only succeed after you have refused to lose hope. The breakthrough might be just around the corner. Persist past the point where you're ready to quit. As someone said, "When you reach the end of your rope, tie a knot and hang on."

However, in other situations you may have to change conditions to ensure your success. If you're in the wrong relationship, job, or you have a problem boss, you should consider cutting your losses and seeking better conditions. It's futile to try to grow in the wrong environment. Don't grind yourself down by staying in an environment that lessens you. Find one that adds to you, and you'll be much happier.

Coping Is Easier for Mature Adults

Face your adversity as a mature adult and you might find it less stressful. Conversely, immaturity can aggravate a problem with irrational expectations or actions. Maturity is a great asset during tough times because you can deal more effectively with the real world of imperfections such as; you, your job, spouse, co-worker, friend, neighborhood, the economy, or the weather. Maturity is your emotional shock absorber for the potholes and rough spots in life. With maturity you can assess the problem as rationally as possible and then act or adjust accordingly. You understand the importance of solving problems and not just complaining about them.

Cope by Keeping Negatives Out

To avoid being negative when you're under pressure, consider how ships remain afloat. They stay seaworthy by keeping most of the water out, and they have bilge pumps to discharge any that enters. Similarly, your mind is a "water-tight" compartment, and its challenge is to keep negative thoughts out. You might be susceptible to those occasional negative thoughts that can seep in. If you don't discharge them, they can affect your ability to keep your head above water.

With thought and discipline, you can learn to control your mind as you do the channels on television. Like the click of a remote control device, you can switch your mental channels. You can select thoughts or moods that are positive, happy, and fun, or negative, sad, and depressing. You choose what you want to see and experience in your life. A speaker at my high school said, "You might not be what you think you are, but, what you *think…you are.* Moods are conscious choices, and, since misery is optional, why would you or any rational person choose to be miserable? Stay positive by keeping the negatives *out.*

Cope by Avoiding the Drain of Negative People

Unfortunately, there are plenty of negative people around. I've known many individuals who seem to actually enjoy wallowing in self-pity over their bad breaks. In their case, adversity seemed to offer a convenient excuse for lack of success. They spent more time telling everyone how hard they had it, than on solving their problems. Most of us recognize the difference between legitimate grief and self-imposed martyrdom. We can try to help the martyrs, but if we can't, we need to avoid them because they can drain the positive feelings from our emotional battery.

An automobile battery loses its charge when there's an electrical short in the system. Likewise, certain people are so negative that they can drain your energy. You might be susceptible to the negative influences of others, and you can experience a sharp drop in energy around those "downers" if you don't watch it. For example, negative friends, relatives, and associates can kill more of your dreams and aspirations than can your worst critics. Well-meaning advice from those close to you can be deadly if it's based on fear and negative thinking. This doesn't mean you become so stubborn or proud that you ignore good advice that can help you avoid major problems. You determine your destiny by sorting through the many advisory messages of care and caution. Only you can decide which voices and messages will influence you.

Despite Adversity, Choose to Be Better for the Experience

Although we experience adversity as part of life, successful individuals cope better than others who allow negative conditions to dominate or control them.

Effective people bounce back from setbacks and address the sources of their frustrations. If life were too easy, it would probably be boring. We need challenges to sharpen our skills and foster our growth. In each adversity there is opportunity. Can you see the opportunity for growth and learning in your current difficulties?

Chapter Six

Problems as Opportunites

Successful individuals have learned that "problems" can lead to opportunities. However, many others still complain about problems and try to avoid them. This blindness to the potential opportunities in problems is widespread. This chapter can help you learn to see the potential opportunities in the problems around you.

Grow from Your Problems

You can be more effective and successful by capitalizing on the opportunities in some of the very problems that would ordinarily only frustrate you. You can distinguish yourself from those who see only "problems" in problems. Despite the negative implication of *problems*, challenges help you grow. Like exercise builds muscles, problems can develop your skills. You can become decisive, persistent, patient, confident, and more effective by successfully handling problems. You can also learn to control the labels you use to describe people or activities that affect you. You can improve your skills and advance your career by proving you can resolve thorny problems.

There are many opportunities in problems. For instance, each item in the local hardware store was made to solve someone's problem. Even in many other fields, one person's difficulty becomes another person's career. Medicine has many examples, from headaches to serious illnesses, where the search for a cure provided new opportunities for individuals and companies. In your case, the marketing advice to "Find a need and fill it" certainly applies to the various needs in the problems around you.

Labels Define Your Problems and Your Reality

You probably don't realize how frequently you use labels to describe problems, yourself, others, or events. You might have used some of the following labels: "I'm such a...," or "He's a real...," or "She's just a...." Your potential for labels is limited only by the number of people you meet and your range of experience. Even the word *problem* is a convenient label to describe a range of irritating or inconvenient occurrences. Although real problems are plentiful, many others are artificial. They are just mislabeled as problems. Use more accurate labels, and you can eliminate some of your problems just by definition. You call the shots on your issues. In effect, you're the umpire behind your home plate. When challenges are thrown your way, they are meaningless until you "call them" and give them a name. Your calls are your labels, and if you control them, you have more control over your moods, your emotions, and your life.

Labels are used so frequently because they're handy for quickly categorizing people, activities, or events. Meaning, nuance, and intent are readily communicated through labels. Labels are the fastest way to express a bias or prejudice; they are simple and quick, but often misleading or wrong. Regrettably, stereotyping is easier due to the availability of simple labels to create categories. There are many single word labels to categorize people by religion, ethnic group, occupation, region, appearance, education, or lifestyle. You've probably heard most of them, and they generally aren't flattering to the subject individuals or groups.

When you label yourself or others, you "accept" the implied definition, emotional message, and artificial limitation of the label you use. For example, if you call someone a "jerk," you don't have to draw a picture to explain your meaning. Although the description may be wrong, the label is absolute; it's all-or-nothing and excludes any middle ground. In the above case, the person is either a jerk or not a jerk. You haven't allowed any other qualities to be considered in the person's defense.

Your emotional reactions will follow your labels, whether you label yourself or others. For example, you've noticed others becoming upset when they use exaggerated terms to describe traffic, weather, their golf, job, spouse, boss, or other people. Also, you'll hear co-workers occasionally describing some of the *routine* requirements of their jobs as problems. I once worked with a supervisor whose favorite word was *problem*. Daily, you could hear him say, "We have a problem. She's a problem or he's a problem." No wonder he was stressed most days. He was adding unnecessary weight to his load by defining routine issues as problems. Some of his problems were actually positive, due to the success of the company. The company was growing and expanding versus the real problems of layoffs and office or plant closings.

You can make your life and work easier by not creating problems where they don't exist. Just avoid mislabeling work, people, or events. Why drive your blood pressure through the roof by mislabeling someone or something? For example, a flat tire is just a flat tire; it's surprising and frustrating, but it's not a world crisis. Instead of telling yourself that the traffic is horrendous, describe it as bumper-to-bumper, perhaps normal for rush hour. The weather is not terrible; it is raining, snowing, or the temperature is eighty degrees. Instead of describing your golf game as a disaster, just recognize the basic fault as a slice, a hook, or a tendency to leave putts short. Deal with what is and don't add fuel to the emotional fire with inaccurate and unnecessary labels.

Watch your labels because they determine your reality. Be a careful umpire in calling life's pitches. They might not be anything until you call them, but they become—in your mind—what you label them. To change your habit of labeling, try avoiding labels for a week. Become conscious of how many you're tempted to use. Eliminate unnecessary emotion and judgment from your statements. Instead, just describe what happens as accurately as possible. You could say, "I burned the toast," or "I was late with the report," or "I made an error in the budget." If you control the accuracy of your descriptions, you avoid triggering negative self-talk and feelings that erode your self-esteem, alienate others, or aggravate issues and make them more difficult to resolve. Give your temper and your adrenalin a rest by using more accurate and less emotional descriptions.

Problems as Stepping Stones

Problems can either be stepping-stones to fulfillment and opportunity or heavy millstones around your neck. Your perspective and attitude determine which they will be. If you view difficulties as normal, then you can grow by accepting and dealing with them. Conversely, you don't develop as much if you have a life of ease. Like a diamond, you don't sparkle by being polished with a soft, silk cloth. You need abrasives to polish your facets. Life provides this abrasive for those that understand its value. It's your choice whether it grinds you or polishes you.

Problems Might Have Created Your Job or Profession

Your position probably wouldn't exist if there were no problems. Frequently, in work, education, and in many other areas, value is often assigned to those who can handle difficult issues or questions. The degree of difficulty you can handle often determines your worth. Your promotion, advanced education, or additional training should qualify you to handle even tougher problems. Usually, when you're promoted, it's not to an *easier* position. However, with the right attitude, you can welcome promotions, problems, and difficult assignments, because you can develop faster and advance more quickly.

Certainly, tough assignments involve risk, but you can significantly strengthen your confidence by mastering difficult challenges. Remember the following statement, and you might not look at problems the same way again. Problems provide your opportunities for growth, but *easy* jobs don't last as long or pay as well. Perhaps, you can afford your current lifestyle thanks to your problems at work.

See beyond the current problems. Use them as stepping stones, and you can grow and advance in a world filled with opportunities mislabeled as problems.

Chapter Seven

Handling Reality More Effectively

How do you handle reality? Although you probably see much that is routine, occasionally, you can receive a serious, unexpected shock. Your experience might match that shared by one of my former associates. He said that most surprises don't involve *good* news. Despite surprises, disappointments, and setbacks, you can learn to handle reality more effectively. If you can accept that something has happened, you are more likely to resolve it or adjust to it. Otherwise, you can continue to feel miserable because you haven't acknowledged that something happened, and that your situation has changed.

It Really Happened: Deal with It

Regardless of what has recently happened, you are where you are and who you are, and you "own" the issue or situation to be resolved. You can't dodge reality, and you have to start where you are when it happens. No matter how painful, or how badly you regret the present hardship, it's your reality. Reality doesn't care whether the cause was your fault or fate; it's just there. Neither wishing nor denying can change what happened. If you've had bad luck, made bad choices, used poor judgment, or failed to care for your job, business, finances, health, or relationships, you must face the consequences as they exist right now. Consequences usually follow behavior, but, even if it's not your fault, the pain and the reality are still there. Absorb the pain, deal with the issue, learn from the experience, and move on. It's not easy, but you can do it.

Initially, many people refuse to acknowledge that something unfortunate has happened, and they expend valuable time and emotion in unproductive anger or denial. Some anger, grief, and sense of loss are normal following a setback. But, life moves on, and we have to recover and start responding.

Successful people tend to handle reality more effectively than others who are less prepared. The reality confronting achievers is no easier for them than the reality facing anyone else. Mature achievers just deal with it differently. They change the reality if they can, change how they feel about it until it's acceptable, or they separate themselves from the reality by leaving a job, changing their career, ending a relationship, or moving to a new location. Despite their frustration or pain, they persist until they deal with the difficult situation.

Reality Interrupts Our Lives and Plans

Reality rarely happens when it's convenient. But, we can deal with it or learn to accept it. However, ignoring reality usually doesn't work. We can create an even worse situation if we if we fail to address the current misfortune. For example, if your car engine starts to knock, and you don't have it checked, the cost and extent of repair will increase in relation to your delay in finding a mechanic.

Are you experiencing a setback or misfortune? If you are, it can be difficult. But, no matter how badly you feel over what's happened or what emotions it triggered, when your tears dry or your anger fades, your reality is still sitting there like an 800 pound bear waiting to be fed. You might delay, but, eventually, you can't avoid dealing with your "bear." Facing your issue may be painful and frustrating, but it's healthier than trying to escape it. Actually, the ability to address reality is a positive sign of mental health. Conversely, one of the characteristics of mental illness is difficulty in dealing with current reality. You can't run away from a reality that's inside your head. Stay with it until you resolve it or accept it.

Asking "Why Me?" Doesn't Help Resolve the Issue

When faced with an unpleasant or difficult reality, you don't help yourself by asking, "Why me?" or moaning, "Woe is me." You haven't been targeted for special hardship since reality often occurs at random. When your reality happens, the most effective response is to determine *how* you will deal with what is. As a coach said after a loss, "When you lose, get back to work. Sometimes, defeat is nothing but education on the way to better results." If you do lose, at least don't lose the lesson.

Our frustration with reality is often based on the belief that something should not have happened, or that something should have happened and didn't. *Shoulds* are meaningless after the fact. For example, if your car breaks down on the way to work, you only waste more valuable time by dwelling on what your car should have done. Further, *shoulds* can only influence results *before* the fact. An analysis of what should have happened might provide some lessons for the future, but it can't alter the current situation after the fact.

Treat reality as just another issue to be addressed. Don't waste time complaining that life isn't fair or easy. It is the way it is. Change what you can and accept what you can't. If you can't, or won't, change your situation, then change your attitude. You'll be happier and more effective with a more "realistic" view of reality.

Chapter Eight

The ABC'S of a Better Life

A B C D E F G H I J K L M N O P Q R S T U V W X Y Z

Look at the alphabet for a minute. These letters have allowed you to read, to learn, and to communicate. However, standing alone, they are meaningless. But, in combination, they can be powerful tools for achieving more happiness and success. These letters have influenced you and enabled you to influence others with them. By arranging them differently, you can achieve an even better life.

While twenty-six letters seem too few to communicate so much, they constitute the primary alphabet in many countries. The hidden power of this scrambled row of letters is *what* you choose to spell with them. This same principle applies to languages with different alphabets. Combination is the key.

From your birth announcement to your obituary, these letters shape you and chronicle your existence. They are the letters of your life. You've already selected those that reflect your journey to this point. Your choices have determined how your life now "reads."

Those choices started early. For example, many of us learned our alphabet while playing with small, lettered cubes. We combined the individual blocks to create words. We didn't realize then that these letters would become the building blocks of our lives.

After combining the letters to this point in your life, are you pleased with the results? You're fortunate if you are. However, if you aren't satisfied, you can change by combining the letters into more positive and effective words.

If you prefer to type your thoughts, goals, and plans, you face the scrambled letters on your keyboard as follows:

QWERTYUIOP

ASDFGHJKL

ZXCVBNM

You have to combine them into meaning. Every keystroke is your choice to communicate with yourself or others. The choices are endless. For example, you can combine them to communicate the following: love, condolence, congratulation, anger, frustration, complaint, litigation, resume, resignation, article, book, proposal, or a speech. These letters have led to love, war, and just about anything in between. How are you combining your letters? Are you directing your life or is it sitting there like the unorganized letters on your keyboard, waiting to be combined into something meaningful?

While we were still young and impressionable, our parents and teachers combined many of our letters for us. Unfortunately, many well-intentioned parents and teachers planted the seeds of negative self-images for some children with the frequent use of such words as; *no, don't, can't, bad, stupid, clumsy, messy, stop,* or *shut up.*

Some individuals continue their negative conditioning as adults. They still replay early memory tapes that reinforce these words: *no, caution, can't, don't, avoid, safe, fear, guilt, inadequate, loser, failure, dull,* and *boring.* Are you still playing some of your mental tapes?

You can change your negative conditioning by changing the words you use to meet your needs. The letters are always available, and you can rearrange them as you wish. Those who've turned their lives around have selected different words to guide them. These "conversions" have occurred in such diverse areas as religion, education, addiction, health, weight, conditioning, career, wealth, and self-image. Some of those new words are: *OK, love, forgiveness, good, change, choice, hope, faith, belief, possible, yes, can, positive, happy, risk, achievement,* and *success.*

Over the next few days, keep track of the key words that you use frequently. Are they positive or negative? Do they reflect hope and confidence or fear and uncertainty? Because you repeat the guiding words so often, they control your thoughts, attitude, and accomplishments in every area of your life. Choose to use the ones you want because what you spell is what you believe you can achieve.

Your tools, the letters from A to Z, are at your service. Your pen or keyboard is there. Convert the alphabet into your vocabulary of happiness and success. Spell your way to a better life.

Chapter Nine

Perspective on Work and Career

Perspective about your work is important to success. Without perspective, competence and intelligence are sometimes not enough to assure a bright future. Many individuals who were smart and talented weren't successful in some jobs. Some didn't succeed because they didn't seem to understand the realities of work or their responsibility for their own satisfaction and success. As a result, their performance was unacceptable in those positions that didn't work out. Others failed because they allowed their immaturity, pride, or stubbornness to override their judgment, blind them to reality, or block helpful feedback they needed.

After observing many individuals struggle with their work, I came to appreciate perspective and its influence on career success or failure. Some of that perspective is included in this chapter, and it's intended to help you be more effective and successful.

Most Companies Don't Recruit at Gunpoint

During my work life—starting in my teens with part time jobs—I've observed hundreds of employees, from clerks to senior executives, responding to the pressures, frustrations, and rewards of their jobs. As an army officer, and as an executive with three corporations, I've seen just about every reaction—including suicide—to the challenges and frustrations of work. Some employees prospered by accepting and enjoying their work, while others would have you think they were recruited at gunpoint, or that they had accepted their jobs as alternatives to prison. Their resentful, negative, cynical, or passive attitudes could almost convince you that their organizations recruited them by force and kept them chained to their desks or company cars. They seem to feel that they had little control over their destiny, and most of them didn't realize the power they had to change their situations. Many were in their situations because they had not prepared themselves for better or more suitable positions. Some seemed resigned to remaining in place until they retired or were forced out. While dreading their work, they looked forward to quitting time or weekends when they could do what they enjoyed.

When I resigned my commission after completing my tour in Vietnam, I started as a trainee with a major corporation. As I rose through the ranks, I noticed the difference in attitudes at each level of the organization. You could clearly see which employees would move up and which ones were stuck where they were. Their attitudes and self-images made the difference. Some, clearly did not see themselves moving up and understood and accepted their status. This group included some employees who recognized their limitations and others who weren't willing to pay the price. The latter accepted the trade-off of promotions, compensation, and—even the loss of their jobs in some cases—for time with the family, hobbies, or other activities that were meaningful to them. In an ideal world, there wouldn't have to be trade-offs, but the reality is that many jobs demand a very high commitment of time and energy for success at work. Balancing success at home is the challenge for many employees.

There were others in the company, however, who couldn't accept their lack of career progress, even though their co-workers were well aware of their attitudes and limitations. Often, these frustrated employees would blame their lack of advancement on politics, or the fact that their managers didn't know how good they were and didn't appreciate them. In many cases, these individuals lacked the give-and-take skills of communication, didn't know how to get their needs met, or couldn't adapt to the organizational environment. In addition, some of them had unrealistic expectations of their bosses or organizations. Most supervisors, managers, executives, and their organizations—like the rest of us—aren't perfect either. However, lack of perfect bosses and organizations doesn't prevent millions of employees from adjusting to the organizations that pay their salaries.

Some of the employees who are frustrated at work don't ask for what they want and become upset when they don't get it. They aren't mature enough to live with *reasonable* imperfections of people and organizations. By reasonably imperfect, I don't mean a bad organization that would cause any normal person to complain or leave. But, even in many "normal" organizations, negative employees can't adjust and don't understand the system or how to progress within it.

I inherited a number of these demoralized or disgruntled employees in units or offices I managed. In some cases my predecessors had been fired or demoted. There were morale problems in those offices. Since there were so many unhappy employees when I arrived, I could clearly see the difference between those with legitimate complaints and those who chose to be negative, despite the efforts of the new management team to address their concerns. The latter were *negaholics* (Negaholism is a term coined by Chérie Carter-Scott to describe a very common condition—the addiction to negativity and self-doubt).

Since my challenge was to turn the operations around, restore morale, and achieve successful operating results, I had to quickly redirect the attitudes and perspectives of many employees. Part of this chapter is an outgrowth of those experiences. Some of these observations might help you personally or assist you in managing others.

We Work as Consenting Adults

I learned some valuable lessons from the painful and frustrating efforts to change the attitudes of the negative and cynical employees I inherited. There was a pattern of thought and behavior among those disenchanted employees. They were reacting like frustrated children who had not learned to satisfy their needs in a constructive manner. They didn't recognize their roles as consenting adults in their current predicament or their responsibility for improving their own attitudes and prospects. They saw themselves as helpless children, while "they" (adults in management) determined their fate. One executive in another company saw this same childish attitude among her staff. She said that she was tired of running an "adult" day care center at work. Some of the childish employees had been conditioned from an early age to passively allow others to direct or control them. They had learned to be helpless.

No Extra Pay for Complaining

I clearly remember one particular employee who was complaining so much when I arrived as the new manager that I finally asked to see his pay stub. Puzzled by my request, he reluctantly showed it to me. I told him that since he was complaining so much on company time, I thought he must have been paid extra to do it, since he did it so well. Although I had not seen a company reward an employee for a negative attitude, I wanted to see how the payroll department was coding his special pay. He got the point.

I also asked him how much he thought the other employees were being paid to listen to him complain. He had not understood that a negative attitude had no economic advantage for him or the company. Sooner or later, this type of employee is asked to shape up or ship out, because no sane supervisor, manager, or executive wants to actually pay someone to make life more miserable at work. If you're paying someone at work to make your life more difficult, think about it. If you're choosing to be miserable and causing problems for your boss or others, think about it. It's not worth spending your life that way when you have other options.

Challenges Are Normal, but Misery Is Optional

The employee who complained so much failed to realize that misery is optional, and that life is too short to be miserable. Write, "Misery is optional," and place it where you can see it daily. It's that important to remember. You should not have to tolerate, endure, or dread your work. You do have options. You've chosen to be exactly where you are, and you can choose to change again if necessary.

You Are Responsible for Where You Are

To help change some of the negative attitudes I inherited, I questioned some of those who were the most frustrated. My questions were deliberately exaggerated to make the point of personal responsibility. If you have a negative attitude about your work, think about your answers to the following questions:

- First, are you in your position by choice or were you recruited at gunpoint? Did the prison bus drop you here as part of the work-release program? Do you reinforce your choice each morning when you walk through the office door? Are you free to leave at any time? Who controls your decision to stay or leave?
- Second, are you volunteering your time here, or are you being paid for your work or profession? Do you consider your presence here a civic duty or a paying job? Do you need the money or is this just your idea of leisure time or a hobby?

- Third, do you understand the level of performance required of your job? Did they explain the expectations and type of work, or were you forced to take it without knowing the requirements?

Surprisingly, some of these employees had not recognized that they were working as consenting adults and were responsible for their situations. Further, they didn't seem to realize that they could change their attitudes or situations if they desired.

In your case, I would add that if you realize you're where you are by choice and reinforce your choice daily by returning to your desk or station to accept your pay, then what's the problem with your attitude? Don't demean yourself by complaining about the choice that *you* make each day to voluntarily go to work. When you're tempted to feel like a victim at work and think you "have" to do what you're doing, remind yourself that slavery was abolished in this country. Freely choose your work and your attitude.

Further, you normally enter the organization at your level of confidence when you apply for a position or are recruited. For instance, if you felt qualified as an executive, manager or supervisor, you wouldn't normally apply for a position that paid much less. In effect, you seek the entry level that you believe matches your skill, knowledge, and experience. It's not the fault of your boss or the organization if you chose a lower position due to your lack of confidence or lack of options. You are responsible if you haven't prepared yourself for a higher paying job. If you want to improve your skills or knowledge, you can do it, but you have to take the time and do the work. You can't wish your way to success. An old English proverb captured this point in these words: "If wishes were horses, beggars might ride." Progress has a price, and you have to be willing to pay it. I've seen many people pay that price and become successful while many of their associates remained behind and complained about their lot in life. What sacrifices are you making to improve? Don't lessen yourself by complaining, when you can do something about your gripe. It is up to you. Do it.

Sometimes, however, there are valid reasons for taking a lesser position, such as; you are returning to work after years away and you need the experience, you are just starting out, you don't want the responsibility of supervision or management, you need the medical benefits, or you need the hours that match your schedule. Whatever your reason, if you're satisfied with your choice, then it's a good decision for you.

When you accept your adult responsibility for the spot you're in, you might develop a different attitude. You could still want to stay with your organization, unless you have an incompetent or abusive boss or you're in an environment that refuses to respond or to change. But, even then, don't blame your boss or the organization if you're unhappy. You hold the key to your satisfaction. You can choose to accept the imperfections of the situation, work to change them, or leave. You have a big stake in making your job work for you and your organization.

But, if your situation isn't working, despite your best efforts, remember that you are in charge of yourself, your career, and you must believe that you deserve better before you can change. You will postpone a better future if you keep thinking: "Maybe, I'm not that good, " or "Perhaps, I can't find another job." Instead, build your confidence and make the change. Convince yourself that you're good and then act like it.

If you cannot change the conditions that affect you at work or alter your attitude to accommodate your situation, then every day that you delay leaving is your fault. If you put off leaving, the more your frustrating condition can erode your self-confidence and morale. However, when you stop blaming others for your situation, it's easier to see that your choices have contributed to some of your problems. With a different perspective and a change in attitude, you might not need to leave. I've seen employees on the verge of being fired, wake up, change, and then earn promotions following major improvements in attitude and performance. Their environments didn't change, but their attitudes did.

To help you view your work differently, the following suggestions and observations can add to your perspective about career satisfaction and success.

Take Charge of Your Career

Your boss is neither your parent nor your entertainment director. Some employees seem to turn their lives over to their bosses or to their organizations. They seem to say, "Manage me or just take care of me." To avoid this, you need to maintain control of your career and not leave your destiny to anyone else. Some employees feel that the boss is totally in charge of their morale, and they aren't aware of their own responsibility to work their job to their advantage. Take charge of your job, but don't hesitate to seek and use advice and counsel. You can always use help, but don't give up control of your initiative, agenda, and plans.

Your Reputation Is Your Career Insurance

How do you insure your career? Although many insurance products are available, you can't buy one to protect your career. You can purchase insurance for life, health, auto, home, business, worker's compensation, and many other risks, but you can't find one for your career. You are self-insured in this key area, and you have to manage this risk yourself. Until you become financially independent or own your own company, your reputation is the closest thing you have for long term protection of your career and future.

Reputation becomes very important when you move beyond your unit, office, division, or company. Since most people don't know your background or get to personally observe your diligent work or your sterling character, they usually hear about your ability, performance, results, and personality from others. Your reputation starts with your internal networks and expands around you as you progress. As your reputation grows, the wider your circle of influence will be. Recruiters certainly know how important a reputation is to an individual's success because that's how they hear about most candidates they don't already know. Your reputation is a combination of attitude, credentials, performance, competence, and the perception others have of you, either from personal experience or from comments about you.

Your reputation stays when you leave an organization, and it provides a bridge to your future if it's good, or a deep, smelly moat if it's not. If your reputation is poor, your former associates are usually glad to see you go, and your future co-workers won't be excited to see you coming. They have probably already called others who know you. It's a small world within industries or professions, in terms of reputation, and it doesn't take long for someone to check you out. Manage your reputation carefully and don't take shortcuts with your work ethic or integrity. Don't wind up like some unfortunate employees. Despite their impressive resumes, they cannot overcome their poor reputations. You can enhance your reputation by giving your organization your best support and performance as long as you voluntarily accept its pay.

How is your reputation? Are you described as "great, good, dependable, terrific, nice," or with some negative comments? A poor reputation is hard to shake and is a heavy liability to bear. However, if your reputation is great, you are very fortunate. When your performance is superior and your attitude is excellent, others will help make your reputation by going out of their way to tell others about you. You should also remember that they can help spread a *bad* reputation just as fast. But, if others don't recognize your name when they're asked about you, you might need to raise your profile within your organization or profession.

Make Yourself Lighter to Lift

We are often dependent on others during our careers, and we can owe much to their advice, help, and care. They can "lift" us within our company or the industry if we earn their support. Make yourself lighter to lift by treating others with respect, regardless of their rank or status within the organization. Most of us are not smart enough to identify only the right people to impress. We've seen cases where unexpected career help came from the most unlikely individuals. Also, employees rise within the organization or the industry, and they can have long memories about slights and favors along the way.

Success is difficult enough to achieve without making enemies who would be glad to put in a *bad* word for you or to worship the quicksand you walk on. I've seen the careers of ambitious people derailed by adverse comments from former associates to recruiters, potential bosses, or other influential individuals. These career-stopping individuals still held grudges or unfavorable views of their former associates' behavior or conduct, even in other companies.

In terms of relationships, remember that you might cross paths with those folks again. It's common to receive calls about someone being considered for a position or for a promotion. How many times have you responded, "I don't know the person, but I've heard...."? Thousands of these calls are made to check on people every day. Many individuals are helped and many are hurt by what the respondents say about them. In addition to treating others with respect, get them in the boat with you and they will be less likely to make a hole in it. Make yourself lighter to lift; get others in the boat with you and they will be glad to help you advance. Try to imagine that five minutes after you've dealt with someone that they received a call seeking information about you. Also, consider—and this has happened many times—that shortly after you met with one of your people, they received a call from a search firm trying to recruit them. Your treatment of them might make the difference in how they respond to both calls.

Maintain a Realistic Attitude

A positive—but realistic—attitude can be invaluable in your career. If you work in an environment that's based on merit, as opposed to family, politics, bureaucracy, or autocracy, your attitude is probably a major asset. However, if you work in some family businesses, and, if you're not "family," you might learn that that blood relationships do matter. Under those conditions, you might not advance, even with a great attitude.

If you work in a political environment, *appearance* might be more important than substance or actual performance. Some politics exists in most companies. You just have to decide if you're comfortable with the degree of political posturing required in your organization. Further, if you're usually upbeat, but find yourself becoming cynical because of the work environment, you should question if it's worth staying there. Your attitude is too valuable to waste in the wrong environment.

If You Leave, Learn from the Experience

If you have an autocratic or an abusive boss, you'll probably leave, unless you like having your self-esteem battered until you believe you're not good enough to work anywhere else. If praise is a foreign language to your boss, and you only hear feedback when there's a problem, you might be wise to examine your career options.

Sometimes, despite your competence and attitude, you might have bosses who are not bad, per se; they just don't match your chemistry, values, or approach, or they might want their own person in your spot. When some managers or executives are new to the organization, or if they feel vulnerable, they might prefer friends, former associates, or other kindred spirits around them for comfort or security. These situations are common, and if you're not one of the chosen few that's just reality in some organizations.

You obviously won't be pleased if you're not chosen, but you can't afford to personalize situations over which you may have little control. However, if it doesn't work out, be honest in assessing your own deficiencies that might have contributed to problems with your boss. Also, leave with some lessons to aid you in the future. Many managers, executives, and professionals have experienced setbacks and disappointments in their jobs and careers. The smart ones learn and become wiser and better as a result. Whatever you do, don't allow your defenses around your ego to block the lessons you need to learn from the adverse experience. If you don't learn from the experience, you risk carrying your "baggage" to the next job and repeating your mistakes.

But, don't linger too long while learning. Cut your losses early and seek the right climate for your beliefs, philosophy, and attitude. Move toward situations that add to you and away from people or roles that diminish you. Remember Mark Twain's advice: "Keep away from people who try to belittle your ambitions. Small people always do that, but the really great make you feel that you, too, can become great."

Refuse to Be a Victim

Avoid being a helpless victim at work. You are there voluntarily and are free to come and go as you choose. You are not an indentured servant who has no chance of freedom for years. Unfortunately, some employees are on a boring treadmill at work and are trying to *exist* on the ten to thirty percent of their job that they like. As a result, they dread or tolerate the remaining major portion of their work. This imbalance is such a waste of their time, energy, spirit, and their life. It's unfortunate that so many employees feel they have no options but to endure their work.

If you're enduring your work and feeling sorry for yourself, remember there's no position description within your organization for a *martyr*. So, don't become one or allow your friends or associates to lose sight of their responsibility and power of choice.

You can find a new position more to your liking. Admittedly, it's not easy to switch organizations and there are risks, but thousands of successful career changes occur daily. Only you can decide if the potential rewards are worth the risk of transition to another division or company. However, don't consider leaving until you can look yourself in the mirror and honestly say that you've done your best to make your current situation work. It's too easy to rationalize your own shortcomings while blaming all the problems on management, systems, or co-workers.

Have you ever changed companies and found similar problems at the new location? As a seasoned manager once observed, "You can be happy or unhappy if you leave or happy or unhappy if you stay." As I was leaving one company to join another, a senior executive I respected said to me: "Other organizations have their problems too." He was right, because there are no perfect organizations. But, if you should find one that's nearly perfect, you can almost bet that it will change.

Almost as soon as you get to the new organization, the person who recruited you could leave, the company could be sold or restructured, and you could be facing even more difficult problems than you left behind. Additionally, you could find yourself among strangers when these changes occur, and you wouldn't have a base of support yet. Despite this risk, don't be afraid to leave; just don't take leaving lightly. The time, effort, and reputation you've invested with your current organization might be more valuable than they appear at the moment.

Create a Better Position Where You Are

Consider the following approach, and you might not have to leave. If you don't like the position you have, perhaps you can create the job you want, right where you are. I saw this concept applied successfully by some individuals in the midst of a major corporation that had detailed organizational charts at every level. This approach can work because your bosses aren't usually spending their valuable time trying to *limit* the scope of your work. Too many people just assume that their job description—if they even have one—sets the limit and scope of their work. The position is not set in concrete and can be altered. Think about how you could expand your position, and you might be amazed at your success. If you persist with a thoughtful recommendation, you might just get it approved. What do you have to lose? Why not try it as an alternative to leaving?

Ask for What You Want

Just ask and you might get what you want. But, don't ask and you're absolutely guaranteed not to get it. Wayne Gretzky, the legendary hockey player, made a similar point in his oft-quoted statement: "Statistically— 100% of the shots you don't take, don't go in." Muster your courage to ask and go for it, even if you're usually reluctant to speak up. Since organizations don't employ psychics to determine what employees want, you have to communicate your wishes and preferences by asking for what you want. It's sad to hear another employee lament: "Didn't they know I wanted that job?" Apparently "they" didn't know of the person's job preference, and they gave the position to someone else. If you ask and don't receive, you're no worse off than when you started. But, you could be much better off if your request were granted. You can win by asking but lose by passing. In addition to asking for what you want, try to understand what your boss or the organization wants. Meeting those needs will help you get more of what you want.

Understand the Contest You're In

"It's hard out there." How many times have you heard a statement like this from fellow employees, as they complained about market conditions, the competition, slow growth, or the economy? After hearing so many complaints from highly competent employees over the years, I finally concluded that some didn't seem to understand the contest they were in, or that they had chosen their type of work for a living. Basically, we're operating in the free market system of capitalism. It encourages the survival of the fittest and weeds the weak and ineffective over time. If we choose to participate, it can be challenging, even though no one promised it would be easy.

Sports provide good examples of choosing one's contest. Athletes vie with each other under the most trying conditions. They compete despite the mud, blood, cold, heat, pressure, pain, and fatigue, and they obviously enjoy the challenge. In sports, you won't see a boxer complaining that the other guy is trying to knock him out. Further, have you ever observed a football player, tennis player, golfer, marathoner, or an Olympic athlete complaining that the other competitors were also trying to win? You probably won't see any, because athletes relish the tough competition, and they've chosen to train and compete at that level.

We need to remember that this same level of competitive intensity exists in business and in other fields. We only magnify our frustrations when we believe that conditions should be easier than they really are. If we don't have the stomach for tough competition, maybe we're in the wrong job. Remember that what we're doing is exactly what we've chosen to do.

To put this in perspective, compare your work to sports. You can use any sport, but consider baseball, for example. There are many levels of play, from a game in the neighborhood, all the way through high school, college, minor league, and the majors. The requirements for ability and mental toughness increase significantly at each higher level, and many players don't make it through the ranks to become major leaguers. In business, however, the levels of performance are sometimes not as conspicuous as those in professional sports. Television, including instant replay, certainly adds to the pressure on highly visible players and teams. Also, thousands of booing fans provide instant, emotional feedback on performance.

Although I've worked with many individuals at various levels of business, I've seen some that didn't seem to understand the need for the same demanding performance required of professional athletes. Some managers and executives just couldn't see the difference in expectations.

I was living in Boston when the Celtics were on top. Their outstanding performance was fresh in my mind as I counseled one of my managers. I told him that he had to decide at which level he wanted to perform. Although he was well paid as a professional, he didn't seem to see himself in that high performance zone. I told him that we could not afford to have him perform with less effort or effect than would be required on a professional team. The rest of the team couldn't carry him.

Professionals need to perform at a higher level. How about you? In which league, or at what level, would you place your attitude and performance? Push yourself to be a major leaguer in your work. Believe me, it's a different mentality.

Be Better than Your Replacement

One key to success is to think of yourself as a professional. Another one is to perform your job better than your potential replacement. As a check against your own performance and objectivity, you can identify what you believe that the "best" replacement would do differently in your position.

Then you can make those changes to strengthen your performance and results. Many who fail know what needs to be done, but they don't act until it's too late, and then they are terminated or demoted. Further, some supervisors, managers, and executives know they need to replace weak or ineffective subordinates, but they don't, and they are replaced instead.

You can avoid this by maintaining your contrast between what is and what is needed and acting on those differences. Maintaining your contrast is key, because when you start to accept less than the best performance, you've lost sight of acceptable standards. Think about your standards and comparisons. They're important, because when mediocre work starts to look OK, the downward drift has started. Stay ahead of the power curve, and you'll address the issues before your boss has to bring them to your attention. Perform so well that your position only becomes open when you're promoted, you retire, or you choose to leave.

Push Yourself to Grow

In a merit environment, you will probably earn your salary between eight a.m. and five p.m. and earn your promotions between five p.m. and eight a.m. Burning the midnight oil on study, reflection, and preparation will give you an edge over the employee who doesn't read or try to improve. It is basic, but, to get ahead, *you* have to do the work. As a professional athlete commented, you can't get someone else to *practice* for you. The employees who don't read, think, or try to improve usually wind up working for those who do. Also, many "former" employees didn't bother to upgrade their skills to meet the changing demands of their jobs.

You don't need the perfect job to succeed, since the opportunity is in you and not in the job. For example, you can get promoted from the same position that your predecessor was fired from. The job is neutral; you make the difference. Change your attitude and you might see more opportunities around you. You can be creative and make more opportunities than you find. It's amazing what you can still discover or learn, even after you think you know it all. Be open to new knowledge. When you learn, you don't just acquire more knowledge. You can become a different person as a result. Also, avoid the easy, comfortable way, because the path of least resistance doesn't lead to success. Push yourself to grow. You don't need someone else to push you or tell you it's for your own good. By then, it could be too late to save your job. Do it before you have to.

Be a Survivor during Corporate Changes

Corporate mergers and acquisitions—often followed by downsizings and layoffs—have become more frequent. There are no guarantees you won't be affected if your organization is involved, but your attitude can make a big difference in how you fare. In the turbulent waters of corporate restructuring, I've seen positive employees float like corks and negative ones sink like lead weights. The negative employees had poor attitudes and couldn't adapt to the new realities following restructuring. The hard fact is that changes are occurring at an accelerated rate. If you're affected, you don't have to *like* what's happening, but you do have to deal with it. It's your reality. Give it your best shot and try to adjust. If you can't adapt, then plan and control your own exit strategy.

Deal with "What Is" and Don't Wait for Fairness

When you discard the notion that life or work should be fair, you will have passed a major milestone of maturity. I feel sorry for individuals who are still waiting for some imaginary ruling body to render a verdict of fairness on various, disappointing setbacks. Some of what happens is just cause and effect, and you will make more progress by concentrating on these two key elements than by wasting time and effort complaining that "It isn't fair." Only the helpless complain, and only the naïve expect fairness. When you don't feel helpless, you are so busy "doing" that you don't have time to complain. It's usually when you feel blocked or stymied that you start to complain. Refuse to be helpless or naïve.

Accept the imperfections of life; they might slow you down occasionally, but they don't stop you from accomplishing your goals. Keep moving in the direction of your goals, and don't get sidetracked by unproductive thoughts or behavior. Refuse to allow yourself any excuse to fail, just because there are some obstacles in your way. Regardless of your frustration, you cannot complain your way to happiness, wealth, or greatness. It's more productive to get over your anger and frustration, get past the obstacles, and get on.

Your Job or Profession: Choose to Like It or Leave It

Perspective about your work and your responsibility can make a difference in your effectiveness. Choose what you do and where you are. Consider your work important and strive to improve your knowledge and performance. Since your organization is paying you, be a professional while you're employed there. Make a habit of going the extra mile and doing your job better than expected. View yourself, your organization, and your work positively. Your attitude can determine your self-image, reputation, performance, position, status, and compensation.

However, if you cannot put your heart into your job or your organization, then get out and follow your instincts to a better match for your interests, skills, and values. Life is too short to drift and dread. Another Monday is coming. It's your life and your choice. It's time to act before you're convinced that you can't leave.

Chapter Ten

Feedback: Seeing Yourself though Others

How are you really seen by others? If you don't know, you risk being a legend only in your own mind. You need feedback on your performance and behavior. Without feedback, you can be so out of touch that your relationship, marriage, or job can be threatened before you have a clue. It's easier to be surprised or stunned by unexpected feedback than you think. Feedback can help you discover your vulnerable areas before it's too late.

Although you may have access to your organization's grapevine and think you're connected to all the key networks, you are probably excluded from the one where you're the subject. If you don't believe this statement, start checking with your friends and associates. In time, perhaps they'll tell you what they're telling others about you. If you're willing expose yourself to feedback, it can open your eyes.

How Do Others See You?

What do your friends, relatives, co-workers, and others say about you when you're not present? If you were a fly on the wall and could hear their comments about you, would you be surprised and pleased or disappointed and hurt? If their comments were favorable, you are fortunate, because you probably have a good feel for their opinions of you.

However, many that receive feedback are both surprised and hurt. Some are shocked to hear, "I'm moving out and filing for divorce," or "Your services are no longer needed." Others are so blind to feedback signals that they are stunned when the crisis occurs. It might have been preventable earlier, but now it's too late. For example, I still remember a sad case from the past. One of my managers came to me on a Monday morning, and he was in bad shape. He looked disheveled and exhausted. On the prior Saturday morning, he answered his front door and found a deputy sheriff waiting for him. Without his knowledge, his wife had filed for divorce and wanted him out.

As the deputy waited to escort him, he barely had time to gather some clothes before he was "out." As he stepped off his porch for the last time, he realized he was homeless. As his home faded in the rear-view mirror, he had no idea where he would go or what he would do. He swore to me that his wife had not even hinted that she was unhappy enough to divorce him. I had a hard time believing that some of her frustration had not registered with him, but, by then, it was too late.

Feedback Is Friendly if You Listen in Time

That divorce raises another issue related to feedback. One concern is when you don't receive the feedback you need. But, another important aspect is when you aren't listening and responding to the criticisms and suggestions you do receive. I've seen too many cases where people who don't listen, don't last. If you don't respond to the warning signs in time, you can damage your relationship, marriage, job, or even your health.

For example, I remember two managers who were fired after repeated feedback about their approach and performance. One, whose people hated him, said as he departed, "My wife says I'm too good to people." The other, who was fired for serious operational and morale problems, said on the way out, "I thought management was my strongest area." The ability to rationalize our mistakes or shortcomings is remarkably strong. Dale Carnegie acknowledged this tendency in *How To Win Friends & Influence People* when he wrote that "...ninety-nine times out of a hundred, people don't criticize themselves for anything, no matter how wrong it may be." Many people will refuse to admit that the problem was their fault, or that they even played a role in it.

Although some feedback can hurt, much of it is friendly since it's intended to help you improve in some area. Also, when people are not officially required to give you feedback, they have to care about you to risk hurting you with comments you need to hear. You need to know they care, because it's possible to trigger your defense mechanism, and have you either clam up or retaliate with observations about their shortcomings. Others react similarly if they feel attacked. They will just defend themselves more vigorously, even if they know you are right. It takes a big person to say, "You're right" when your feedback is interpreted as criticism. But, when feedback is given in a caring, helpful manner, it's easier for the other person to acknowledge it.

You should expect some discomfort when you seek honest feedback from others. When they help, they invest some of themselves in you, and want you to succeed. If they see that you're responding to their feedback, they will defend and praise you to others and assist you in other ways, if you're open to advice and counsel. Your supporters can be invaluable in helping you improve and become more successful. They provide an invisible safety net to help protect you, and they look out for you, even when you aren't aware of their efforts. Let them help you. A request for help is a powerful magnet to attract support.

Take the Initiative in Seeking Feedback

Why don't you receive more feedback? You might already be receiving it, but maybe you aren't "tuned in." The more likely reason that you aren't receiving enough is that you aren't seeking it. Friends and associates don't want to hurt your feelings and risk jeopardizing your relationship, or they might think it's useless to comment because you don't indicate any desire to change. Also, some others are reluctant to give you feedback under any circumstances, because they haven't been trained or encouraged to provide it to anyone in the past.

Provide Feedback to Others as You Seek Your Own

You are probably typical of those who are uncomfortable giving feedback to others, unless you are so mad that you don't care about their reaction. For example, how reluctant are you to advise friends and associates that: they have bad breath, body odor, food on their face, or spinach in their teeth? How comfortable are you telling them that their perfume or after shave lotion is offensive, their fly is open, their slip is showing, or their hair and clothing smell from smoking? Could you tell them that they're considered too opinionated or obnoxious? You see some of these feedback possibilities every day, but, if you're like most people, you're reluctant to say anything to the person involved. Although some of the feedback can be embarrassing to them, it may be worse if they don't know about it.

Years ago, one of our employees was embarrassed by lack of feedback. He walked around the office with his fly open and his white shirt protruding through the zipper. Finally, another employee informed me, and I advised him. Naturally, he was humiliated because someone didn't tell him immediately. This is only one of countless examples where helpful feedback is withheld from individuals who are blissfully unaware they are causing others to snicker behind their backs.

During the day, notice how many comments you hear about others that are not shared with them. How many comments do you think are not shared with you? Ask for feedback and find out how you are seen. Don't let yourself be surprised or hurt by discovering a problem too late to change the outcome. Even on lesser matters, don't let yourself be ridiculed because you're oblivious to your behavior, manner, appearance, or dress. Become aware through feedback.

Change Can Begin with Awareness

Assuming we want to change, we can only change when we're aware. When we don't seek others' views of us, or they don't give it, we are denied the opportunity to correct our faults or flaws. In some cases, what we don't know about ourselves can hurt us. As indicated earlier, if feedback is provided soon enough, it may save a marriage, relationship, or career. Some people are surprised to discover that their friends and co-workers actually appreciate the feedback they receive. People do want to know, if the feedback to them is handled tactfully and carefully. I've often heard comments such as: "I'm shocked; I had no idea I was doing that. Why didn't you tell me sooner? I'm embarrassed that I've been doing this without knowing. Thank you for telling me." A secretary I once knew was humiliated to learn—after working for her boss for three years —that he didn't like for her to chew gum at work. She felt crushed that he hadn't advised her in the beginning. Unfortunately, important feedback is withheld in too many cases. For example, are your friends and associates tolerating something about you, or are they itching to give you some feedback? Why not ask them and find out?

To paraphrase the saying that "Friends don't let friends drive drunk," I would add that people who care about others don't let friends and co-workers continue to behave in unconscious ways that hurt themselves. It's not unusual for us to say and do things that we don't remember, and we routinely perform these unconscious acts. Body language, for example, often involves meaningful, but unconscious, movements. Because many words and actions are unconscious, people will tend to deny them. Think of your own experience. You've probably heard someone say, when confronted with some statement or action that you observed, "I wouldn't say that," or "I wouldn't do that." They really believe they didn't say it or do it.

I used to hear similar denials from employees requiring feedback on their behavior or performance. Despite the observations of a number of their co-workers that they were behaving in a certain way, the individuals would still deny it. The next time you are tempted to deny a word or deed, try to remember every word you spoke for the last minute, last five minutes, last hour, or the most recent twenty-four hours. Your words and actions become a blur. You can only recall what you meant to say or do or what you thought you did. It's virtually impossible to remember what you *actually* said or did for the hour, day, or week. Believe me, we often act and speak without being conscious. Many arguments and disagreements have been caused by this blindness to one's words and actions. Seek and use feedback to discover your unconscious areas of behavior.

Without feedback, you are unaware of the gap between how you think you're doing and how your friends, family, and associates actually see you. Consequently, it's easy to be hypocritical because you don't recognize the contradiction between your words and your deeds. Hypocrisy is easy to spot in others, but if you aren't providing this feedback to them, how many aren't giving it to you?

Based on your blindness to various aspects of your behavior or performance, you can use some help from your friends and associates. Also, care enough to give feedback to others. If they know you care, they can handle it. Both you and others instinctively know the difference between a caring advisor and a cynical critic. However, even a cynic might express some painful truths that you need to hear, because your friends may be too nice or too considerate of your feelings to "lay it on the line" with you.

Feedback Can Stimulate Growth

Criticism, despite its temporary sting, can stimulate our growth. What hurts can instruct, and we can grow from the pain and introspection. It's better to receive a number of small hurts from feedback than to have our shortcomings accumulate until it's too late for an apology or corrective action. Although it might be unpleasant to hear, we need to seek candid feedback and let our friends and co-workers know they won't hurt our feelings or our relationships by being honest with us. Getting feedback is similar to catching fish. Fish don't jump into your boat, and feedback doesn't normally seek you out. Get out your "hook" and go after some feedback.

Feedback can help change your life by allowing you to respond to wake-up calls before it's too late. With constructive feedback, you don't have to be perfect as an employee, spouse, friend, or in any other role. The reason you don't have to be perfect is that you can change others' perception of you by your responses to their input about your imperfections. You can become almost as good as perfect if you eliminate your shortcomings based on their suggestions.

Life Is Smoother with Feedback

Think of feedback as your social and behavioral wind tunnel. The wind tunnel is used to refine a design, to reduce friction, drag, noise and vibration. Feedback can help you reduce stress and friction. It can also help polish your rough edges and minimize turbulence in your relationships. If you are receptive and responsive, you can have a smoother passage through life because others will help "shape" you along the way.

Earlier, I noted the advantage of grabbing your job by the smooth handle. Unfortunately, there are still too many people who keep stubbing their toes by not understanding what they are doing wrong or why success seems to elude them. They don't understand why they aren't invited to lunch, why they're excluded from meetings, or why they aren't getting promoted. They are getting in their own way because they are not receiving or responding to feedback. Without feedback, they really don't get it.

Get a Free Reality Check

Feedback is beneficial. It's free, but it's not necessarily pain free. It's friendly if you take it and use it in the right spirit. Why not seek a reality check from your friends and associates by asking how you could improve or what suggestions they might have? They will be reluctant until they know you absolutely want their input. Over time, they'll be more inclined to tell you some things about yourself that they would normally only tell others in your absence. Seek feedback. Open yourself to a wider perspective of your impact and behavior. Since you are comfortable using a mirror for feedback each day while shaving, applying makeup, and checking your clothing or hair, why not use others as mirrors of your appearance, behavior, and performance? It's worth the effort and temporary discomfort if you want to grow and be more effective. To grow, you need to know...about yourself. Feedback can put you in the "know" where it counts.

Chapter Eleven

Decision Time

By the time you reach this chapter, I hope you've already decided to change some aspects of your life. But, if you're still wrestling with the decisions that frustrate or inspire you, you're not alone. Sometimes, these decisions take months, or even years, to make. If you're still reading, then you apparently have the commitment to change. If you're serious about changing, then keep trying until you do.

Unfortunately, some have only half-hearted commitments to change, and they conclude that their only option is to endure their frustration. As a result, they bury their dreams and exist in a state of frustration, cynicism, and regret until they die. For some sobering perspective, read a few obituaries in the local papers. Notice how differently the individuals lived and how they were remembered. Also, note that not one obituary indicated what the deceased "could" have done. It's too late for unrealized potential at that point. When your obituary is printed, will it reflect the life you wanted to live? If not, you still have time to change it.

Despite your current situation, you need to believe that change is possible. The possibility of change gives you hope in facing your dreams or dreads. You can change if your pain or your desire is strong enough. You only fail if you quit trying and give up. Life is too brief and precious to merely endure. You can develop the will and the courage to choose a better way. Happiness and misery are homemade.

I hope that you are ready to clear the final hurdles and reach your decisions. Since we couldn't meet face-to-face, I've tried to appeal to your inner feelings and to motivate you to change. You are special and you can "live" your valuable life.

You've probably heard someone say that after all is said and done, more is said than done. Don't allow this statement to apply to you. Act on your convictions. In finding your courage to act, remind yourself that many have overcome situations more difficult than yours, and they were able to change and find happiness and success. What they have done, you can do. You already know what you need to do; you just need to do it. The only force stopping you is you. You control the only voice telling you that you can't, and you command the powerful voice saying that you can.

There are answers for you. You have the same twenty-four hours and the identical twenty-six letters that others have used to change their lives. Decide what you want and focus your time and effort to achieve it. Give yourself permission to change and to live a special life. As I wrote in the Introduction, don't let your epitaph read, "I could have, but I didn't." Do it!

After finishing the book, if you still can't make those key decisions, then reread some of the chapters. Eventually, perhaps, you'll make those choices. Believe that you are special. Realize the miracle of being the *one*. Have the courage to walk through your mental door to a better life on the other side. Live your one life. It's up to you. Change your situation and—for a change—start looking forward to Mondays.

About the Author

Sam Daniel Jr. has been a military officer and a senior executive in business. As a leader, he has worked with employees at every level of various organizations. He has led and mentored employees, from entry level to presidents. He has spoken at conventions, workshops, seminars, and other meetings, on motivation, leadership, self-development, management, and communication. He lives in Williamsburg, Virginia, with his wife, Robbye.

Appendix

Additional Reading

Anderson, Walter. 1986. *Courage Is A Three Letter Word*. New York: Random House, Inc.

Brande, Dorthea. 1936. *Wake Up and Live*. New York: Cornerstone Library

Bristol, Claude M. 1948. *The Magic of Believing*. New York: Cornerstone

Burns, David D. M.D. 1980. *Feeling Good*. New York: Avon Books, Inc.

        1990. *The Feeling Good Workbook*. New York: Plume

        1993. *Ten Days To Self-Esteem*. New York: William Morrow and Company

Carnegie, Dale. 1936. *How To Win Friends & Influence People*. New York: Pocket Books

        1944. *How to Stop Worrying and Start Living*. New York: Pocket Books

Emery, Gary, and Campbell, James. 1986. *Rapid Relief from Emotional Distress*. New York: Rawson Associates

Foundation for Inner Peace. 1975. *A Course in Miracles*. New York: Viking Penguin

Harvey, Joan C., with Cynthia Katz. 1985. *If I'm So Successful, Why Do I Feel Like A Fake?* New York: Pocket Books

Helsmstetter, Shad. 1982. *What To Say When You Talk To Yourself.* New York: Pocket Books

Hill, Napoleon. 1965. *Think and Grow Rich.* New York: Hawthorne Books, Inc.

Maltz, Maxwell. M.D. 1960. *Psycho-Cybernetics.* New York: Pocket Books

Mandino, Og. 1982. *Og Mandino's University Of Success.* New York: Bantam Books
                  1990. *A Better Way to Live.* New York: Bantam Books

Peck, M. Scott. 1978. *The Road Less Traveled.* New York: Touchstone

Reaves, Chuck. 1983. *The Theory Of 21.* New York: M. Evans and Company, Inc.

Schuller, Robert H. 1983. *Tough Times Never Last, But Tough People Do.* New York: Bantam

Schwartz, David J. 1959. *The Magic Of Thinking Big.* New York: Fireside
                  1983. *The Magic Of Getting What You Want.* New York: William Morrow and Company, Inc.

Carter-Scott, Chérie. 1989. *Negaholics.* New York: Villard Books

Stone, W. Clement. 1962. *The Success System That Never Fails.* New Jersey: Prentice Hall

Index

can't afford to personalize, 79
answer(s)
    are within you, 25
    related to timing or conditions, 53
    anticipation, life without, 6
ask/asking
    for what you want, 26, 81
    how you could improve, 94
    might get what you want, 81
    muster your courage to, 81
    usually reluctant to speak up, 81
    win by, 81
athletes
    have learned, 16, 47, 50, 56
    relish the tough competition, 82
    train and compete at that level, 82
attention, 9-10, 19, 84
attitude
    at each level of the organization, 69
    is key, xiv, 30-31, 33, 35, 37, 84
    of gratitude, 45
    major asset, 30, 78
    made the difference, xiv, 9, 69
    no latitude on attitude, 38
    pave your way or block your way, 30
    ways to improve your, 34
avoidance
    becomes your choice by default, 22
    only postpones the problem, 11
aware/awareness
    can only change when we're, 91
    of the messages you receive, 17